# A ZERO WASTE LIFE

## IN THIRTY DAYS

# A ZERO
# WASTE LIFE
## IN THIRTY DAYS

### ANITA
### VANDYKE

VINTAGE BOOKS
Australia

*This book has a durable cover that is designed to last. Keep it, share it and pass it on. To recycle, just take off the front and back cover and put the book in a paper recycling bin. The planet will thank you for it.*

A Vintage Australia book

Published by Penguin Random House Australia Pty Ltd Level 3, 100 Pacific Highway, North Sydney NSW 2060
penguin.com.au

Penguin
Random House
Australia

First published by Vintage Australia in 2018

Addresses for the Penguin Random House group of companies can be found at global.penguinrandomhouse.com/offices.

 A catalogue record for this book is available from the National Library of Australia

ISBN 978 0 14379 1 379

Cover illustration by kirpmun/Shutterstock
Interior images: line drawings by Louisa Maggio; watercolour illustrations by Melissa Stefanovski; hand drawn lines by Marie Smolej/Shutterstock
Author image by Joi Ong
Cover and internal design by Louisa Maggio, Penguin Random House Australia
Printed in Australia by McPherson's Printing Group

Penguin Random House Australia uses papers that are natural, renewable and recyclable products and made from wood grown in sustainable forests. The logging and manufacturing processes are expected to conform to the environmental regulations of the country of origin.

# CONTENTS

*To my family,*
*who taught me to not waste my life.*

# INTRODUCTION

This book is a practical guide designed to help you reduce your waste by 80% in thirty days. It's also a reflection on how I became an accidental environmentalist. It tells the story of how I went from being a maximalist to a minimalist, from 'hero' to zero – to living a 'zero waste' life.

I didn't grow up with a hippie mother or a passion for the environment, I was just a person trying to find happiness in all the usual places – money, power and status. But this triumvirate of success didn't provide me with the happiness that I expected. I was *wasting* my life.

But how did this journey all begin? What is living a zero waste life? I'll start from the beginning. My 'aha moment' as Oprah calls it.

It all started with a simple no. Standing at the supermarket checkout, the cashier looked at me and asked 'Would you like a plastic bag for that? It'll be an extra 15 cents.' A plastic bag for 15 cents? Sounded like extortion to me. I had just quit my job the previous day and I needed to make ends meet on one income. That first no, based on economics rather than environmentalism, was over two years ago, and since that day I've said no to plastic bags over a thousand times. I've also said no to disposable coffee cups, fast fashion and excess consumerism. And in saying no to all this, I've actually said *yes* to a whole new life. That first no led me to a zero waste life.

───

*How did I end up here?* Crying at a dining table in suburban Sydney, surrounded by my mother-in-law's Royal Doulton porcelain figurines. It had been another terrible day at work and I'd come home to an evening sorting the many boxes of stuff we'd brought with us to my in-laws' house, where we had recently moved in an attempt to pay off our debt. The dam had burst and I didn't know how to stop. All I could think was 'how did I end up like this?'

On paper my life was the epitome of success. I was the one my parents didn't have to worry about: the daughter who graduated high school with a near perfect UAI, had a well-paying corporate job and the latest Givenchy boots in my closet. It was a supposedly picture perfect life.

My parents brought me up believing that money was essential to happiness. Poor immigrant workers who never had any money, they saw it as the solution to all their problems. So I did what many a good, first-born daughter of a Chinese-migrant family has done and worked hard, got good grades and then a high-paying job. I climbed the corporate ladder, foregoing my passions, hobbies and creativity to chase the Great Australian Dream.

By age twenty-six I was a manager in a large engineering firm, earning more money than my parents ever had. The day of the 'broken dam fiasco' was just another day at the office. I remember sitting in that Board Meeting on Level 6, looking at my boss, my boss's boss and the big boss, thinking *Is this it? Is this who I will become in five, ten, fifteen years' time?* I realised then that if I kept going down this path, all my hopes of living a life that was truly mine, one that wasn't bound by golden handcuffs, would be lost forever.

A more profound question followed: *What did I want to do with my life?*

These questions haunted me and when the doubt started to make me miserable, my husband looked me in the eyes and said 'You have to quit your job – it's killing you.' Of course, being the practical, money-driven person I was, I had a dozen excuses. We needed to pay the mortgage. We couldn't afford to live on one income. We needed the money. But my husband was adamant. I knew then that if I didn't do something about my everyday misery, I risked losing him.

I quit my job the next day.

Since that day, my life has transformed. By embracing a zero waste life, I have been able to go back to university to study full-time to become a doctor, I've moved out of my in-laws' house into a 59-square metre apartment and I've dedicated my life to something greater.

Working in corporate Australia didn't reflect who I was, but that doesn't mean it's not right for everyone: you certainly don't have to quit your corporate job to live a more eco-friendly life. But you do have to find what works for you. Living a zero waste life means more than just a plastic-free diet – it gives you the freedom to live in alignment with your values. To live a life based around service, community and respect for the planet we live on. It has allowed me to not waste my life.

There is a stereotyped image of the quintessential environ-mentalist: a left-wing hippie who doesn't wear deodorant and lives off-the-grid. But I want to introduce to you a new kind of environmentalist: the 'everyday activist'. Being an everyday activist is about valuing small and consistent actions, the compound effect of which can not only reduce your waste but also enrich your life. I want to show you small changes can make a big cumulative difference.

Zero waste is the ultimate goal, but there's no need to feel daunted. Quite simply, zero waste living is about leaving a gentler footprint on the planet. That's it.

This is an interactive book that gives you the power to be an activist in your everyday life. I have chosen a thirty-day timeframe, as research has shown that it takes approximately thirty days to develop a new habit. My engineering brain has 'hacked' each day to make it as simple as possible. Cumulatively, the daily tasks transition you into a zero waste life. Your journey comes in two parts, and focuses on four stages of change – think, do, reflect and review.

## DAYS 1-15: THINK & DO

The 'think' stage involves an initial audit of your life: assessing your current baseline so you know your starting point, opening your eyes and being curious about living a more eco-friendly existence. The 'do' phase involves the delta – in engineering terms this means the change that is required. The first fifteen days ask for action; they're about making simple changes that set you up to live a zero waste life.

# DAYS 16–30: REFLECT & REVIEW

These final fifteen days involve introspection, as well as an inspection of your external environments. They are about recognising the *why* of change rather than the *how*. The last fifteen days will give you the passion to fuel long-lasting, sustainable change.

The aim of this thirty day challenge is to show you that living zero waste is not about deprivation or sacrifice. It's just a few creative swaps that transition you to an 'eco-luxe' life. I still wear designer shoes (second hand, of course), I enjoy nice things (all plastic-free) and I live a busy life in the inner suburbs of Sydney. The key to living a sustainable life is that it has to be sustainable for you. That is why for each 'action day' I've created the *three steps to zero waste* method. This method provides you with three options:

1. Reduced waste
2. Low waste
3. Zero waste

This means you don't have to start with the zero waste option straight-away – you can gently ease yourself in. It also gives you the chance to 'level-up' and increase your commitment across a timeframe that suits you. Engineered to give you flexibility and freedom, this method is designed to allow you to mix and match different options to suit your different circumstances.

Living a zero waste life is not only actually really easy, it is also completely *necessary*. We can all be environmentalists, regardless of which political party we vote for, because we all need to be caretakers for this planet we live on. We all need to lower our environmental footprint, not for altruistic, bleeding heart reasons, but because Earth is the only home we've got. It is for purely *selfish* reasons that we need to reduce our waste, because our very existence is tied to the fate of our planet.

This book is for the everyday activist in all of us, who wants to continue living without sacrifice or deprivation. It is about how we can say *no* to waste but *yes* to life.

Through the next thirty days, I hope to show you that by living a zero waste life, you actually gain more – more time, more money and more life. Isn't that what we all want in the end: a life of happiness, a life of luxury, a life that isn't wasted?

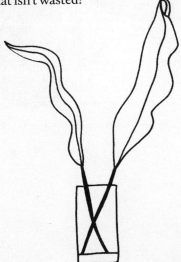

# THINK & DO

———

DAYS

1 – 15

# DAY 1

# START WHERE YOU ARE

---

When I started my zero waste journey the state of the environment was the last thing on my mind. I had just quit my job and was trying to make ends meet for two people on a single income. I began the journey not to save the planet, but to save money. I could only afford to buy the essentials, which forced me to question every purchase and get creative with my limited budget. Since then, I've discovered so much about the environmental impact of waste and my motivations have gradually changed. I have come to understand that we need to leave a gentler footprint on the planet, because Earth is the only planet we can call home. But without that initial financial incentive I wouldn't have made the decision to start.

# WHY DO YOU WANT
# TO LIVE A ZERO WASTE LIFE?

Is it to save money? To reduce your environmental impact? Are you curious about what living a zero waste life means? Perhaps you're tired of not having any control over the state of our planet. Today is about making a commitment: to think about yourself, and to be open-minded and curious about the changes to come.

Take 5 minutes to write down why you're trying out a zero waste life.

These are just some of the initial reasons for starting your zero waste journey. By the end of the thirty days, you'll have a dozen more.

# ENVIRONMENTAL FACTS TO GIVE YOU A KICK UP THE BUM

## Did you know?

1. Shoppers worldwide use 500 billion single-use plastic bags per year – that's about a million bags per minute across the globe.

2. Every piece of plastic created since the 1950s still exists.

3. At least two thirds of the world's fish population is suffering from plastic ingestion. Think this doesn't affect us? We eat fish and drink the water that we are dumping our plastic into.

4. Plastics are made of petrochemicals. These chemicals leach into our waterways and enter our food chain.

www.plasticpollutioncoalition.org

# CREATIVITY WITHIN CONFINES

I want to introduce you to the concept of 'creativity within confines'. Being an engineer is essentially being a professional problemsolver. Before we start any engineering project, we are given a brief, which is an outline of the problem at hand, including a list of 'confines'. Using creativity and brainpower, we then engineer a solution to the problem.

I suggest you apply the same creativity to zero waste living. The confines are that we can't use plastic and want to find the most eco-friendly solution possible. Let your creativity blossom within these confines!

# DAY 2

# DO A BIN AUDIT

---

I was inspired to do my first bin audit after seeing a talk by aquanaut Dr Sylvia Earle, one of the first women to explore the depths of our oceans. I had always considered space the final frontier, but her talk made me wonder why we always look towards Mars when we haven't fully explored the 70% of our planet that is underwater. When Dr Earle explained how plastic pollution was choking our sea life and waterways, I knew I had to do something. She suggested not using disposable plastic bottles as a good first step. Simple, I thought. Even I can do that!

That night I opened Pandora's box. Pulling plastic bottles from my smelly bin, I also saw styrofoam containers, food scraps, disposable coffee cups, napkins, plastic cutlery, plastic bags.

I started separating items into a recycling pile and then became confused — can you recycle cling wrap? I was literally a rocket scientist, but I couldn't figure out which containers were recyclable. Houston, we have a problem.

Doing a bin audit is powerful because it shows you the reality of your waste, and what habits you personally need to change. It's an assessment of the 'ins' and 'outs' of your waste, an opportunity to analyse what comes into your home and understand where your waste goes. It's your chance to assess where you are before implementing new changes to reduce what you send to landfill. Let's begin!

# HOW TO PERFORM A BIN AUDIT

1.  Put on a pair of gloves and lay out the contents of your rubbish
    bin on some newspaper. Ideally, you should do the bin audit
    before your garbage collection day to see the full extent of
    your household waste.

2.  Categorise your items into similar materials – paper, plastic,
    food, glass, aluminium, unidentifiable. Unidentifiable items
    may include electrical goods and mixed packaging.

3.  Find out what can and can't be recycled in your area by
    Googling your local council + 'recycling'. Print this list out and
    put it above your bin as a reference for everyone in your house.
    Note what the unidentifiable items are – we will investigate
    mindful recycling and disposal options throughout the next
    thirty days.

4.  Examine your buying habits. Is your rubbish mainly
    food waste? Coffee cups or take-away food packaging?
    What do you buy most frequently?

5. Note down the 'frequent flyers' in your bin. We'll take a closer look at some common frequent flyers in days three and four.

6. Brainstorm how you can make simple switches to replace your disposables with reusables. Most often, the key is to avoid creating waste in the first instance. By reducing your 'ins', you also reduce your 'outs'.

# ZERO WASTE HACK!

## Bin liners

Three alternatives to using plastic bin liners:

1. REDUCED WASTE Buy compostable bin bags made from cornstarch, which are readily available in supermarkets. These cost slightly more than plastic liners, but you won't need to buy as many because you're about to start drastically reducing the materials you put into them.

2. LOW WASTE Line your bins with newspaper. Yes, that's right - newspaper! By composting most of your 'wet' rubbish (see Day Four), you'll eliminate bin juices, and newspaper will suffice for your remaining 'dry' rubbish.

3. ZERO WASTE Remove your bins altogether and store your weekly rubbish in a glass jar — the ultimate zero waste status symbol. Limiting yourself to a glass jar worth of rubbish gives you a clear target and makes it easy to measure how far you've come.

# WHY IS PLASTIC SO BAD ANYWAY?

Plastic is made from petroleum, which is a non-renewable resource. Once we've exhausted our fossil fuels, we won't be able to make any more plastic products, yet rather than treating plastic like a precious resource we act as though it will never end.

Before I began my zero waste journey, I didn't really know what plastic was. Everything seemed to have the recycle symbol on it so I assumed it was being repurposed back into the product chain, like metal and glass.

Glass and metal products can be recycled infinitely without degradation in the quality of the material. On the other hand, plastic is not recycled infinitely – it is downcycled, meaning it is recycled into poorer and poorer quality plastic until it can no longer be used. Then it sits in landfill, leaching into our soil, causing greenhouse gas emissions and contributing to climate change. Moreover, most of our plastic rubbish ends up in our waterways, where it has the most detrimental impact. It chokes our sea life and breaks down into microplastics that contribute to a toxic food chain that starts with the small fish, and ends up at the top of the food chain (us).

# DAY 3

# MAKE A ZERO WASTE KIT

---

We live in a disposable society. From the plastic bags given to us for every purchase through to the rise of fast fashion and disposable electrical goods. The single-use water bottle we buy at the convenience store, the plastic straw we use to drink our green smoothie, the disposable cup we use for our daily coffee – every one of these items, all used for less than fifteen minutes, will sit in our landfill for hundreds of years. The math just doesn't add up.

Luckily there is a solution and it is so simple. The first step is to say NO to these disposable items. The second step is to REPLACE these disposables with reusables.

The zero waste kit I have put together consists of the Big Four items that make up an alarming majority of our landfill. I recommend you store them together in a cotton bag that you can transfer from your backpack to your handbag in a jiffy. By bringing this simple zero waste kit with you wherever you go, you will drastically reduce your plastic consumption.

# CONTENTS OF THE ZERO WASTE KIT (I.E. THE BIG FOUR)

1. Foldable reusable bag – so there's no excuse for single-use plastic bags! I use a cotton bag, but any lightweight material will work.

2. Stainless steel drink bottle (glass and metal are better options than plastic as they can be recycled infinitely) – invest in a good quality drink bottle and it'll pay itself off in just a handful of uses.

3. Reusable coffee cup (one with a good seal so it's spill proof) – not only are these great for coffee or tea, but you can also use them to store snacks, like nuts, on the road. No need to pay for an expensive nut bar wrapped in plastic!

4. Stainless steel straw – straws are one of the major landfill pollutants. A handy tip is to say 'no straw please' when you order, and make sure you do this before the drink arrives. Alternatively you can bring your own straw, or even better, just use your mouth and go without one!

# ZERO
# WASTE
# HACKS!

## Three ways to rapidly reduce your Big Four use

1. REDUCED WASTE Just say no! The first step to reducing the Big Four is by refusing straws, plastic bags, coffee cups and plastic drink bottles. If you don't have a zero waste kit with you, go back to basics: use your mouth instead of a straw, ask for a cardboard box or paper bag instead of a plastic one, drink straight from the bubbler instead buying a bottle.

2. LOW WASTE Choose the sit down option. Many disposable items are created for convenience, but does it really take that much longer to sit down and drink your coffee in a café? Choose the eat-in option instead!

3. ZERO WASTE Create a zero waste kit and take it with you wherever you go.

## Your kit can also include

A cloth napkin to replace paper napkins

A reusable cutlery kit – spoon, fork and knife
(or the ever useful spork)

Reusable produce bags for small items

A reusable glass jar to store smoothies, leftovers
and last minute food purchases

# DAY 4

# COMPOST, COMPOST, COMPOST

When I did my first bin audit, I was shocked by the amount of food I was throwing away, and it turns out I'm not the only one. In Australia, over a third of household rubbish is food waste! Let's first talk about where food waste ends up. Remember, when we throw things away, there really is no such thing as 'away'. Rotting food sits in landfill producing methane, which is a major contributor to gas emissions. Moreover, when you waste food, you are also wasting resources — this includes the soil, water, labour and transport energy used to grow food and bring it your dinner table. We need to be more conscious consumers, and stop throwing away our hard-earned money. Food waste is bad for the environment and bad for our bank balances!

# COMPOSTING 101

The easiest way to reduce the 'wet' goods you send to landfill is to compost. I was initially daunted by the idea of doing my own composting – I worried that it would be messy, smelly and attract rodents. But it turns out there are simple solutions for all of these issues, and in the end composting has been one of the simplest switches I've made. Instead of food scraps going into the bin, they go into a compost container. Make sure the container has a lid, and keep it in the fridge or freezer so it doesn't get smelly. Easy! Then it's just about finding the right way to dispose of them – different composting systems have different rules for whether you can include animal matter, such as bones and meat. Over the page are a few simple options, so you can find the right method for you.

**1. REDUCED WASTE** Once a week, take your container to your local community garden, school, nursery, neighbour's backyard or wherever there is a communal compost bin and deposit your compost there. This means no upkeep, no mess, no rodent attraction! Easy!

Google 'local compost bin' to see what is available around you, or just go for a walk to explore and meet your neighbours. I found three compost bins within walking distance of my home. Most people are more than happy to share their compost bins, as composting helps produce a rich fertiliser for their gardens. Just make sure you check to see what rules they have for different organic matter.

**2. LOW WASTE** Compost in your backyard! Local councils often provide discounted compost bins and run workshops on how to maintain them. Here are some home composting tips:

A. Make sure you have a good amount of wet and dry compost. Wet compost is your daily food scraps, dry compost is things like leaves and paper. This is an excellent way to redirect your paper from the recycling bin!

B. Make sure your compost bin has a lid! This prevents rodents from getting into your bin.

C. Rotate the compost every so often — no need to be precious about it, just give it a stir every week and in a few months you'll have great soil for your garden!

## 3. ZERO WASTE Remember, most composting is only for fruit and vegetable scraps. Animal products such as cheese, bones and meat can only be composted in certain systems. For a totally zero waste solution, you can do the following:

A. Use a bokashi bin! This is a special bin that comes with a spray that helps accelerate the fermentation process of food. Unlike other composting methods, you can also put animal products in a bokashi bin, which ferments the scraps and produces a liquid fertiliser you can use on your plants.

B. Have a worm farm — they're excellent for large households as the worms produce rich fertiliser at an accelerated rate. You can't feed your worm farm animal products, but it is a much quicker process than normal composting. I live in an apartment and have a worm farm — I asked the strata committee if we could store it in under the communal stairs and the worms are happy in this cool damp place. Worms are odourless and stay within their farm, so there is no chance of them escaping! They love all vegetables and fruit (except citrus) and are my husband's pride and joy.

# DAY 5

# PUT YOURSELF ON
# A SPENDING BAN

We have been programmed to buy, buy, buy to feel happier, sexier, smarter. But none of these 'things' are satisfying what we really need: purpose, love and joy. We all need to feel like we belong, like we matter, that we are living meaningful lives. Buying everything we want is not going to satisfy what we really need.

It's time to put a stop to the endless cycle of buying objects that placate our small selves. To achieve this we need to respect our resources, including our money, our time and the planet's resources. So today we're putting ourselves on a spending ban, which means for the rest of the month we're only going to buy things we really need.

Putting yourself on a spending ban will help you realise that not only do you have enough stuff, but that you are enough.

# RULES OF THE ONE-MONTH SPENDING BAN

1. No spending on superfluous items. This includes clothing, shoes, make-up, skin-care. No purchases of these items whatsoever, even if they are on sale!

2. Yes to spending money on food and essentials!

3. Yes to spending money on experiences, seeing friends, going to the movies, catching up for lunch. Even better if you can swap these for free activities, such as hiking, going on picnics, having tea at home. None of these activities should require new equipment; just make do with what you have.

4. Know what your priorities are. If you want to see where your values lie, look at your bank account. This spending ban will help you direct your finances towards things that truly matter to you (ironically, they usually aren't things).

5. The rules are essentially 'no new stuff' but it's up to you to define what your focus is. Do you have too many unread books? Do you have piles of clothing with tags still attached? Ten shades of unused lipstick? You decide what you most need to put a stop to.

# THREE WAYS TO HELP YOU SET THE RIGHT SPENDING BAN FOR YOU

**1. REDUCED SPEND** If a month without spending feels almost impossible, why not start with one week? If you're ready to go further, push on for two weeks and then eventually the full month! Some people work well with strict rules, others need incremental steps. The main thing is to set boundaries that work for you!

**2. LOW SPEND** Start saying no to shopping as a social activity! Do you really need to spend your time at the local shopping centre, or could you spend it on a coffee and a walk? What about a movie and a chat with a friend? You'll instantly remove the temptation involved and start to replace shopping with new hobbies. Our culture has made consumption a leisure activity, but this is your chance to take back your time and money and change your habits!

**3. ZERO SPEND** Challenge yourself to a month-long spending ban on everything except for food, water and transport. This means finding alternatives for everything!

- Instead of buying books, can you borrow them instead? Can you organise a book swap or book club within your local community?

- Instead of driving your car, why not walk? Can you try cycling or map a walking route to work? Most people are surprised by how quickly they can cover ground when they give walking longer distances a go. It could be as simple as strolling to the shops instead of driving. Make it part your (incidental) exercise regime!

- Can you borrow a film and hold a movie night instead of going to the movies? Cook brunch for your guests instead of going out?

These are just a few ideas for how to do a month-long 'zero spend'. The zero spend option is a great experiment for those who want to see where their money is going and curb their spending habits. Use a budget app or simply write down your purchases every day, and at the end of each month compare it to the previous one. You'll see exactly how much you have saved!

# DAY 6

# DO YOUR FIRST ZERO WASTE SHOP

Since I started buying produce at bulk stores, farmer markets and local businesses, grocery shopping has become a joy. I take the time to talk to shopkeepers and growers, I've gained a genuine appreciation for food and I get to avoid the 'noise' of excess packaging and the marketing that comes with it.

Some people think that shopping zero waste makes you a nuisance but I've found shopkeepers and customers love when I ask questions and always say they wish more people engaged the same way. In all honesty, initially finding zero waste options can take a bit more preparation, but it's all about working out a routine that suits you. By changing my habits, I have found a shopping routine that balances materialism and environmentalism, excess and frugality, convenience and conscious living. It has allowed me to embrace the confines of a plastic-free life and be creative with simple alternatives that fit into my lifestyle. Remember, consumption should not consume you.

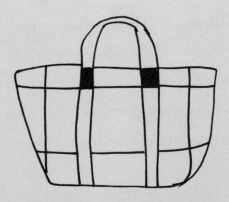

# ZERO
# WASTE
# SHOPPING KIT

1. **REUSABLE GROCERY BAGS** – ideally these should be made of cotton, but use what you have. You can buy more at the end of the month if you need.

2. **REUSABLE PRODUCE BAGS** – you can sew your own or buy them online. Weigh them and write their empty weight on the bag.

3. **REUSABLE JARS OR CONTAINERS** – use any you may have at home. Recycle and use your old jars before you buy anything new!

# HOW TO DO YOUR FIRST ZERO WASTE SHOP

## 1. DO YOUR RESEARCH

- Are there any bulk or health food stores nearby? If not, what is your closest one?

- Are there any farmers' markets? When are they open?

- Are there fruit and vegetable delivery services in your area? What is their delivery schedule?

- Go into your local supermarket. Is there a bulk aisle? What foods are available plastic-free?

## 2. WRITE A SHOPPING LIST

- Take a look in your pantry and plan your meals for the next week. Write down everything you need to buy.

- Plan ahead. Are there package-free options for what you want to buy? What and how many containers or bags do you need to bring?

## 3. GIVE IT A GO

- The first shop is about exploring your options; it should be a fun exercise to get to know what's available and what works for you.

- Check out your closest bulk store. Educate yourself on its protocols, which differ from store to store — you may need to weigh containers before filling them and write codes on jars. Write off your first trip as a learning experience — subsequent trips will be easier and quicker. The shop assistants are usually very helpful and if you have kids, you can get them involved in this more interactive shopping environment.

- Have a chat with the fishmonger or the butcher to explain why you are bringing your own containers. Local businesses are incredibly knowledgeable about their food and are more than happy to help!

You might not be zero waste the first time you shop, but I can guarantee that you'll automatically reduce your waste drastically by being a more conscious consumer!

# HOW TO SHOP AT YOUR LOCAL BULK STORE

These steps may differ slightly from store to store.

## PREP

1. Write a list of all the items you need. I only visit the bulk store every 2–3 weeks. Adapt the frequency to suit your lifestyle.

2. Put together a zero waste shopping kit with jars and produce bags.

3. Bring some extra jars for impulse buys.

## TARE THE JARS (MAKE THE WEIGHT ZERO)

At the bulk store, weigh your containers first thing and write each weight on the outside using stickers or a marker. To streamline the process, weigh every jar right at the start, before you fill any of them – this saves you from going back and forth between the scales and produce.

# FILL THE JARS AND PRODUCE BAGS

Fill your containers with the items on your list. Don't forget to write the code for each item on the container for the cashier. Each code is shown on the bulk bin.

## CHECKING OUT

1.  Make it easy for the cashier – line up your jars and produce bags.

2.  Keep an eye on the register to make sure the weight of your jars is removed from the final weight.

3.  Make sure your lids are screwed on tightly and pack your jars standing up so they don't fall. Using a straw basket helps cushion them.

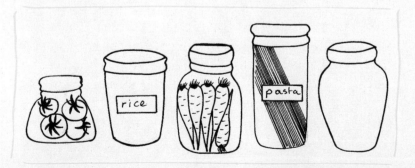

# HOW TO REMOVE
# STICKY LABELS
# FROM JARS

1. Remove as much of the label as possible.

2. Rub the area with a mixture of bicarbonate soda and coconut oil (this loosens the glue used on labels).

3. Wash the jar with hot soapy water and give it a good scrub.

4. To remove any lingering smells, use a 50/50 mixture of white vinegar and water and soak overnight.

# THREE EASY WAYS TO REDUCE YOUR WASTE WHEN GROCERY SHOPPING!

## 1. REDUCE YOUR WASTE WHILST SHOPPING AT YOUR LOCAL SUPERMARKET

- Shop the outer aisles. Fresh produce does not have any packaging.

- Bring your own grocery bags and if you forget, ask for a cardboard box.

- Choose the better option – glass, cardboard or aluminium packaging. If plastic is the only option, buy the biggest size available to avoid excess amounts of small packaging (e.g. buy the biggest size of oats available instead of buying individual microwave portions).

## 2. LOWER YOUR WASTE BY SHOPPING AT A BULK STORE OR FARMERS' MARKET

- Take your own containers to the bulk store, butcher, fishmonger or deli counter when buying meat, fish or cheese. Don't forget to ask the cashier to tare the containers before filling them.

## 3. ZERO WASTE SHOPPING (THE ULTIMATE GOAL)

- Shop at your local farmers' markets. You'll eat seasonally, buy organic and you can suggest to growers you frequent that they reduce their plastic packaging.

- Get an organic delivery box delivered to you. The service I use allows you to return the box, which means no waste whatsoever! It also means that I eat seasonally and buy organic produce at an affordable price. This is a great option if you don't enjoy a regular expedition to the shops.

- Make products yourself. Most of the ingredients you need for cooking and cleaning can be purchased from a bulk food shop and stored for long periods of time, which means shopping can become a once-a-month occasion.

# MAKE YOUR FIRST ZERO WASTE MEAL

I've always loved food, but I didn't use to know much about it.
I wasn't aware of what was in season, what fruit and vegetables
were local to my area or where my meat, eggs and milk came from.
When you put yourself on a zero waste diet, you become a better
cook, even though you have fewer ingredients to choose from.
I call this the zero waste paradox.

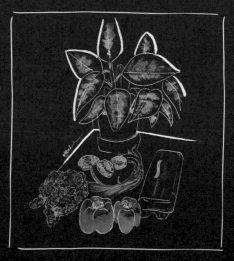

# THE ZERO WASTE PARADOX

The 'creativity within confines' concept is most apparent when it comes to cooking. We have an obsession with food that is reflected in the way we shop and eat. There are an overwhelming number of cookbooks and cuisine types: Mondays you might have an Indian curry; Tuesdays a Chinese stir-fry and Fridays might be Mexican taco night — the choices are endless.

Before I embraced zero waste grocery shopping, I felt scattered and overwhelmed when it came to cooking and preparing meals. The 'zero waste paradox' is that, despite having fewer ingredients to choose from, I've become a better cook. This is because I no longer have decision fatigue. I have 5–10 foolproof recipes that I rotate and make regularly, which means I have mastered these recipes and could pretty much cook them blindfolded. These recipes are made from zero waste ingredients, taste delicious and take the stress out of cooking!

# THREE PRINCIPLES FOR THE ZERO WASTE COOK

1. Avoid food packaging.

2. Eat what is in season.

3. Use what you have.

Let me expand on these:

## 1. AVOID FOOD PACKAGING

This means eating fresh produce, which has the added side benefit of eating a 'cleaner' diet. Have you noticed most heavily packaged items have a huge ingredients list? Not only are these foods encased in plastic, but many of them have deviated so far from their raw ingredients they have become *plastic food*. Embarking on your zero waste journey means eating real food, which is an empowering and liberating feeling. You might even find you lose weight despite eating more, and save money despite avoiding cheap disposable meals.

## 2. EAT WHAT IS IN SEASON

When you understand what is in season, cooking and eating becomes a sensuous affair. We eat with our senses and if our food is packaged in plastic we only get to use our sight. There is nothing more sensuous than running your fingers along verdant bunches of kale, smelling fresh basil and tasting ripe tomatoes. When our food is packaged in plastic, we judge it by sight rather than luxuriating in all our senses.

## 3. USE WHAT YOU HAVE

How many cans of tinned food do you have in your pantry? How many bags of limp salad leaves have you thrown away this week? Food waste is a huge issue in every household. Before we shop for more groceries, let's shop our own pantry and eat down our stores. Do a pantry audit before you go grocery shopping and use what you have before you buy more!

# DAY 8

# PREVENT FOOD WASTE

---

Food waste is a huge problem in Australia. Australians throw out one-fifth of the food we buy each week. Yes, that's right — one-fifth! Produce is so abundant in our country that most of us have never known what it's like to be truly hungry, so we don't think twice about throwing it away when it looks a bit sad, or if it's past its 'best before' date. Our cultural obsession with aesthetics has enabled the disposal of produce due to small imperfections. We expect our food to be blemish-free and the 'right' colour. The United Nations Food and Agriculture Organisation estimates that a third of all food grown gets thrown away due to these imperfections — a shocking statistic!

By throwing away food, we are also wasting the vast quantities of water, fertiliser and fossil fuels used to grow, process and transport produce from grower to consumer. And as we know, rotting food in landfill produces methane, a potent greenhouse gas that contributes to climate change. Our indifference to the problem of rising food waste is a result of the increasing distance between humans and the land in which our food is grown.

Today we break the cycle of food waste.

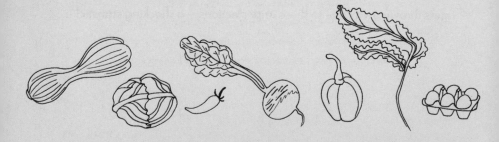

# THREE STEPS TO ZERO
# FOOD WASTE

## 1. REDUCED FOOD WASTE

A. Make an 'Eat Me First' container for the top shelf of your fridge.
   Put all the orphan fruit and vegetables that need to be consumed
   first here. This acts as a home for the food that mysteriously
   disappears in the fridge and is a great reminder to eat these
   items before they go off!

B. Chop up your produce and store it in airtight containers – putting
   in 30 minutes of prep work will make the rest of the week so much
   easier. This is a key tip to save time and food from going to waste!
   Throughout the week you can add your chopped ingredients to
   smoothies, salads, curries. It's also a great way to ensure you get
   enough fresh produce into your diet.

C. Understand the difference between a 'use by' and 'best
   before' date. Best before dates are recommendations from the
   manufacturer for when the product tastes its best – nothing to do
   with when the product actually expires. 'Use by' dates are very

conservative estimates of the time it takes for food to go 'off',
but even then, most products last well beyond this date.

## 2. LOW FOOD WASTE

A.  Freeze your leftovers. If you see your fruit or vegetables getting
    a bit sad, chop them up (if you haven't already) and pop them
    in the freezer for use later.

B.  Shop your pantry. Make a list of the ingredients in your pantry,
    stick it to your door or store it on your phone. Before you go
    shopping, check your list and look up new recipes that will use
    up what's in your pantry. Once again embracing the principle of
    creativity within confines!

## 3. ZERO FOOD WASTE

A.  Store everything in glass jars. Not only is it aesthetically pleasing,
    but it encourages you to use what you have. No more hidden
    packets of rice and boxes of pasta. If you find you need more
    containers, wait until your spending ban ends to buy more – you'll
    likely find you accumulate them naturally as you switch to buying
    produce in glass jars. You can also check out your neighbourhood
    recycling bins, ask friends and family or even buy jars second-hand.

B. Have a Friday mash-up. Before your grocery shopping day, get creative and make a mash-up that uses all your vegetables and other leftovers in the fridge. I like to make egg scrambles or one-pot curries.

C. Be a mindful consumer. A bit of work in the present will save you time in the future.

    i. Do some meal planning.

    ii. Have four to five go-to recipes for leftovers. Choose from your favourite recipe books or do a simple google search.

    iii. Don't buy more than you need.

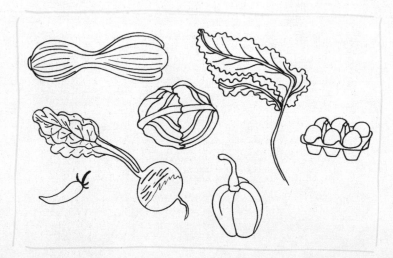

# DAY 9

# DECLUTTER YOUR HOME
# PART I

I used to have a lot of *things*, my closets, drawers and cupboards filled

to the brim with cheap and cheerful finds from my latest shopping

trips. I always believed it was an organisation issue, but it wasn't lack

of storage, it was an excess amount of stuff.

Simplifying your possessions is a key part of living a more eco-

friendly life. If everyone lived like we do in Australia, the UK and the

USA, we would need at least three Earths to satisfy our consumption

habits. We need to slow down our consumption, and the first step

is decluttering our homes. Studying rocket science, we learnt it's

impossible to shoot towards the stars if you're anchored by excess

payload. The clutter in our homes weighs upon us, making our

lives heavier. With our zero waste journey, we're aiming to make ourselves more streamlined and aerodynamic in order to achieve our dreams and goals.

My three-day decluttering method revolves around three areas — clothes, home items and mental decluttering. You can skip ahead to check out the other parts of this decluttering challenge, but each step will require a bit of time — it's my belief that getting rid of stuff is harder to work into your daily routine than buying new stuff. To begin with, let's talk about decluttering our clothes.

# HOW TO CURATE YOUR CLOSET

**1. BEGIN BY REFLECTING** Reflect on the life you live (not the dream life in which you wear kaftans all day and do yoga by the beach!). Your wardrobe should revolve around your *real* life. Decluttering forces us to become *clothing curators*.

**2. PUT ALL YOUR CLOTHES IN A PILE** Take every item you own off your hangers and out of your drawers and washing basket, and put them in one big pile on the floor. Realising just how much stuff you have could come as a shock!

**3. SORT YOUR PILE** Start with *type*, *length* and *colour*. You can further separate your clothes according to the characteristics below:

A.   TOPS By sleeve type, from shortest to longest i.e. sleeveless, short sleeve, ¾ sleeve, long sleeve.

B.   BOTTOMS By length and type i.e. shorts, skirts, knee-length, full-length.

C.   JACKETS AND COATS By length and heaviness of fabric.

D.  DRESSES By length of sleeve and hem.

E.  ACCESSORIES Into handbags, belts, hats, scarves, jewellery.

F.  SPECIAL OCCASION AND SEASONAL ITEMS This can be done last
as you can store some of these items.

## 4. IT'S TIME TO BE RUTHLESS So often we buy clothing for when

we are the 'perfect' size or for a holiday we haven't booked. In reality,
most of us like to be comfortable, practical and stylish in our everyday
lives. Your aim is to keep key pieces of clothing that reflect how you
want to look and feel every day.

## 5. SORT YOUR CLOTHING INTO FOUR PILES

A.  KEEP These are items that match your curated style. Return them
to your wardrobe by type, length and colour. Your new wardrobe
should feel controlled, clean and stylish.

B.  REPAIR Do any repairs immediately, e.g. sew that loose button,
re-stitch that hem. Be realistic — if the repair is too difficult consider
donating or disposing of the item mindfully.

C.  SELL You might come across items that are worth reselling. However, due to the rise of fast fashion, garments depreciate quickly. Be realistic about the time, cost and effort required to sell second-hand clothing. Do a google search to see the 'going-rate' for the brand and item of clothing to see if it is worth your time.

D.  DONATE/DISPOSE Please refer to Day 26 to learn how to upcycle, recycle, donate and mindfully dispose of clothing items.

6. The final (and possibly most confronting) step is to crunch the numbers. For every clothing item you dispose of, donate or sell, write down the amount of money it cost you to buy. Then tally up the costs. Let that number sink in.

Now it's time to move forward. We all need to be conscious of how we spend our money, so that we respect our planet's resources.

# DAY 10

# ORGANISE A 'PROJECT PAN'

———————————
———————————

Project Pan involves choosing ten skincare or makeup products that we continuously use until we 'hit pan', which means using them until you can see the bottom of the 'pan'. This way, you use up your existing products before buying anything new.

The beauty industry is centred on 'quick fixes' and 'cheap hits'. How many times have you been sucked in by two-for-one deals? Beauty products are advertised to fix your skin (and life) problems, but we all know this is a gimmick that companies use to make us feel insecure so they sell more products. In the past I fell hard for these gimmicks – I *needed* a new lipstick to cheer me up after a tough day. But no amount of concealer could hide that what I really needed was a change in my life.

Today we embrace true beauty: beauty that makes you glow from within. Unfortunately, this can't be bought off the shelf. It's time to put an end to meaningless purchases and use up what you have. In the future, if you do need to buy new make-up, you'll make better choices. Project Pan saved me thousands of dollars, and helped me become a more conscious consumer.

# HOW TO
# STERILISE
# BEAUTY CONTAINERS

1. Choose the best-quality containers. Ones made of glass are ideal, or thick, durable plastic that can be reused (better than it being downcycled or going to landfill).

2. Remove the labels (see Day 6).

3. Wash the containers with hot, soapy water.

4. Place in a pot of boiling water for ten minutes to sterilise them.

5. Remove and allow to dry before filling them with your own DIY beauty products (see Day 11).

# THREE STEPS TO REDUCE YOUR SKINCARE AND COSMETICS WASTE

## 1. REDUCED WASTE

A. Put yourself on a cosmetics and skincare spending ban (see Day 5).

B. If ten items seems too daunting, select five items that you'll diligently use for the next month.

C. Get creative using up what you have. Why not use the facewash you don't like as a shower gel instead? If you don't like the smell of a hand lotion, why not use it as a foot cream?

## 2. LOW WASTE

A. Declutter and sort your beauty items. Gather all your beauty and skincare products into a pile. Sort through items that are half-used, still new, etc. Create a pile for those that can be given away or donated. Create another pile for items that need to be used up. Research how you can use up these items creatively, YouTube and blogs are a great place to start. Can you create a new make-up look? Can you mix products together?

B. Shop your beauty box. Whenever you are tempted to buy anything new, look at all the items you already have. Make a list on your phone so you know what you have before you buy anything new.

C. Select ten items for your Project Pan.

## 3. ZERO WASTE

A. This is all about making better choices in the future. Check the ingredient lists on your skincare and beauty products and you'll likely find that many of the individual ingredients are highly toxic. Moreover, many products are tested on animals. There is no need for another animal to suffer for the sake of your beauty. It took me over two years to use up all my beauty products. After that, I replaced everything with cruelty-free and plastic-free beauty products – I even made my own (see Day 11)!

B. Dispose of your beauty packaging mindfully. Many companies have programs that allow you to return your used cosmetics and skincare containers for recycling. You can also try companies such as TerraCycle, which recycles everything, or you can sterilise containers and reuse them.

# DAY 11

# MAKE YOUR OWN BEAUTY PRODUCTS

I'm a messy cook and I don't like to pay attention to precise measurements, so when I first started creating my own beauty products, I knew I had to make them simple, fast and using ingredients I could easily get plastic-free.

Your skin is the largest organ of your body. Most of the ingredients in skincare and cosmetic products are unpronounceable — and you certainly wouldn't eat them! My rule of thumb for beauty products is if it's good enough to eat, it's good enough to go on my body.

My favourite products are now ones I've made myself, from ingredients I have in my pantry. I wish I could share this advice with my teenage self. Think of the money, time and energy I could have saved!

This section contains tips on how to reduce your waste when it comes to skincare and beauty products. I'll also share my favourite DIY beauty product recipes, which can last you months and which you can make again and again.

# THREE STEPS TO MAKING YOUR OWN ZERO WASTE BEAUTY PRODUCTS

## 1. REDUCED WASTE

A. Replace all your beauty products with bars or organic products instead.

    i. Shower gel > use a bar of soap

    ii. Shampoo > use a shampoo bar

    iii. Conditioner > use a conditioning bar

    iv. Moisturiser > use coconut oil

    v. Shaving gel > use coconut oil, also replace your plastic shaver for a metal shaver.

B. Replace your cosmetics with products that are:

    i. Cruelty-free (free from any form of animal testing)

ii.   Palm-oil free (save the orangutans and prevent deforestation!)

iii.  Contain ingredients that you can pronounce. Works for what you eat, also works for what you put on your face!

iv.   Plastic-free. Choose package-free options or try products packaged in glass, bamboo or stainless steel

## 2. LOW WASTE

A.   Dabble in making your own beauty products. Here is my cheat sheet for easy DIY beauty products that give you the best bang for your buck in terms of cost and time:

   i.   MOISTURISER Thick, heavy-duty moisturiser is so easy to make and lasts ages (see Page 67 for my DIY beeswax or cacao moisturisers).

   ii.  BODY SCRUB Did you know that most store-bought body scrubs contain microbeads (plastic beads that act as exfoliants), which end up in our waterways and are consumed by our sea life? Our beauty products should not cost the Earth — literally. Make your own body scrubs with sugar or ground coffee, it's so easy!

iii. COCONUT OIL This really should be renamed 'miracle oil'. You can use coconut oil as a moisturiser, make-up remover, hair mask and shaving cream and it's the most common ingredient in my DIY recipes. Make sure you buy organic coconut oil that is stored in glass, even better if you buy it from a bulk store!

# 3. ZERO WASTE

This 'level-up' option involves making all of your beauty products.

A. COSMETICS These might be easier than you think. I suggest googling recipes and giving them a try. Most recipes cost less than two dollars to make and it's so much fun to experiment in the kitchen with different colours and ingredients!

B. DEODORANT AND TOOTHPASTE Check out my DIY recipes – they may not be for everyone, but I guarantee you these recipes work!

C. SOAP There are so many recipes available online, and making one large block of soap means you can cut it down and even give the bars as gifts. You can also take a workshop on how to make soap.

# MY FAVOURITE DIY
# BEAUTY RECIPES
## FACE

### MIRACLE CLEANSING OIL

This is my favourite DIY beauty product. All you need to do is:

1. Find a 30 ml dropper jar or any jar you can easily fill.
2. Fill half the bottle with organic sunflower oil.
3. Fill a quarter of the bottle with organic jojoba oil.
4. Add 20 drops of organic essential oils of your choosing.
   You can tailor it to suit your skin type:
   - Tea-tree for acne-prone skin
   - Ylang-ylang for dry skin
   - Lavender for combination skin

Shake thoroughly and apply to your face after removing make-up with coconut oil. Massage thoroughly and wipe off with a warm washcloth. The results are amazing!

## EYE MAKE-UP REMOVER

This removes even waterproof make-up. Gently rub your face with ½ a teaspoon of olive oil and wipe off make-up with a warm cotton washcloth. You can also use coconut oil as an alternative.

## FACE MOISTURISER

The easiest way to moisturise your face is with oils. Jojoba oil can be great for combination/oily skin, while rosehip oil can be good for dry skin. Add essential oils such as lavender, tea-tree and ylang-ylang for some luxury – remember, a few drops go a long way.

## TONER

I have two recipes, chosen by skin type.

- OILY/COMBINATION SKIN Use a 1:1 ratio of apple cider vinegar and water, and apply on skin. Wipe with a reusable cotton round or a cotton washcloth. (The apple cider vinegar smell disappears after a few minutes.)
- DRY/SENSITIVE SKIN Use rosewater, which can be bought in a glass bottle from your supermarket (try the international section), or you can soak (organic) rose petals overnight in water. Store in an old, sterilised spray bottle.

# SKIN

## BODY AND FACE SCRUB

This is a recipe for a lemon and bergamot sugar scrub, but you can change the oils according to the different seasons. For example, lemon and lime for summer, or lemon and lavender for winter. You will need:

- 1/3 cup brown sugar (the finer the better)
- a squeeze of lemon juice
- lemon rind (to be ground into the sugar)
- 1 tablespoon of melted coconut oil
- 1/3 cup of olive oil
- a few drops of bergamot essential oil

Mix this all together in a large bowl and decant into a container of your choice. It smells so luxurious and doesn't have any microbeads, like many store-bought body scrubs.

## BATH SALTS

I make a batch of these regularly because I go through them so quickly. You will need:

- a packet of Epsom salts (1 kg)
- herbal tea (I normally use elderflower, but you can use any herbal tea you like. It's also a great way to use up any leftover herbal tea you no longer want to drink.)
- lavender and geranium essential oils

Mix it all together and decant into a jar of your choice. You can decorate the jar with a ribbon and brooch from an op-shop to make it into a luxurious gift. I saw the same product being sold for thirty dollars at a health store, but I made my own for one-third of the cost!

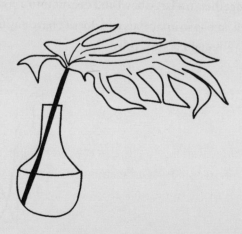

# BEESWAX BODY MOISTURISER

Making your own body balm is very easy and saves you so much money. You will need:

- ¹/₂ cup of olive oil
- ¹/₄ cup of coconut oil
- ¹/₄ cup of beeswax
- 5–10 drops of lime and lavender essential oils (or any essential oils of your choice)

Pour everything into a jug and heat in a pot of water (double boiler method). Let it melt and place the lid on the pot to help the mixture heat up faster (this should take about 15 minutes). Pour the mixture into a jar of your choice.

# VEGAN BODY MOISTURISER

This vegan-friendly moisturiser smells good enough to eat! You need:

- ¹/₂ cup of cacao butter
- ¹/₄ cup of olive oil
- ¹/₂ cup of coconut oil

Pour everything into a jug and heat in a covered pot of hot water for about 10 minutes (double boiler method). Pour the mixture into a jar of your choice. In the summer, keep it stored in the fridge.

## TOOTHPASTE

This may take some getting used to, but it's such a cost-effective way to clean your teeth. You will need:

- 1/3 cup of organic coconut oil
- 1 tablespoon of baking soda
- 10–20 drops of spearmint essential oil
- 1/2 teaspoon of stevia (optional)

Mix this all together and store in a glass jar. You can spread it onto your bamboo toothbrush and brush away!

## DEODORANT

This may need some experimentation and will require reapplying after a sweaty workout. However, it's hypoallergenic and great for sensitive skin. You will need:

- 1/3 cup of baking soda
- 2 tablespoons of coconut oil
- 1/3 cup of cornstarch
- 10–15 drops of essential oils

(I love the combination of ylang-ylang and lavender)

Mix this all together and apply with fingertips or a small wooden spoon.

# DAY 12

## MAKE YOUR OWN CLEANING PRODUCTS

Look underneath your sink. Is the space there filled with cleaning products for every surface in your house? Me too! I had over ten different bottles for my small apartment. Not only is this a waste of space, it's also a waste of money. Moreover, the chemicals used in these industrial strength cleaners are toxic for our planet and for us too. If you have sensitive skin, you'll notice straight away how harsh these chemicals can be.

There is a theory about how overly clean our world has become – it's called the hygiene hypothesis. Nowadays, household cleaners kill 99.99% of all bacteria and gel hand sanitisers are everywhere. The truth is, we need healthy bacteria to ensure the optimal functioning of our bodies. The hygiene hypothesis theorises that the exponential increase in allergies is due to the over-sanitisation of our homes and our lack of contact with bacteria as children.

There is no need to fear everyday germs, our bodies are designed to build immunity to bacteria. The only place where we need to kill 99.99% of bacteria is in hospitals! Let's save ourselves from allergies and save our waterways from being clogged by toxic chemicals — it's time to make our own cleaning products.

# REPLACE EVERYDAY HOUSEHOLD CLEANERS WITH THESE SIMPLE DIY VERSIONS

## ALL-PURPOSE CLEANER

This is a recipe your mum or grandmother might have used. If it worked for them, it'll work for you. It does a thorough job without harsh chemicals!

All you need to do is:

- Fill an empty spray bottle (glass is preferable, but reuse an old spray cleaner bottle before you buy new) with 1:1 white vinegar and water. If you don't have white vinegar, you can use 1:5 apple cider vinegar and water.
- Spray the area you'd like to clean. Then wipe down with rags made from old towels or t-shirts, or a cotton washcloth.
- Add 10-15 drops of essential oils for added scent!

## LEMON/ORANGE ALL-PURPOSE CLEANER (GREAT FOR WOODEN SURFACES)

This is a great recipe using lemon, orange, grapefruit and lime peels. Any citrus fruit will be perfect for it!

All you need to do is:

- Place your used peels in a large glass jar, then fill the jar with white vinegar. Allow it to ferment for 5–7 days (you can leave it for as long as you want, really).
- Drain then pour the liquid into a spray container and add water (1:1 ratio). Spray away!

## CASTILE SOAP

Liquid Castile soap (soap made from olive oil) is truly all you need for your household needs. I refill my liquid soap from the bulk store. If this is not available to you, you can grate a Castile soap bar and melt it into a large pot of boiling water.

Here are some easy recipes using Castile soap – you can add your preferred essential oil:

- dishwashing liquid (1:10 Castile soap and water)
- handwash (1:5 Castile soap and water)
- laundry liquid (1:5 Castile soap and water)
- spray stain remover (1:2 Castile soap and water)

# MORE HANDY CLEANING TIPS

- STAIN REMOVER SOAP BARS You can buy these from the supermarket wrapped in cardboard or paper. They work a treat for hard-to-remove stains.

- BUYING IN BULK Laundry powder/liquid and dishwashing liquid can be bought in bulk stores if you don't want to make your own.

- REUSE YOUR OLD CONTAINERS Plastic spray containers are the best — reusing them also prevents them from ending up in landfill.

- NEVER BUY PAPER TOWELS AGAIN Use old cotton washcloths and t-shirts. Create a rag basket and label it for the household. Use the rags until they get dirty and then just pop them in the washing machine. Easy!

# DAY 13

# SHOP YOUR WARDROBE

_____

_____

My wardrobe was (and still is) my biggest problem area. Both my parents worked in the Australian fashion industry so I grew up with fashion in my blood, and I've always had a real passion for clothes. I understand that we all like to look our best! But looking smart doesn't need to come at the expense of detrimental labour rights, poor working conditions and harm to the environment.

Fast fashion is a term attributed to the rate in which chain stores take designs from the catwalk and send it out into production at an expedited rate. After watching a documentary called *The True Cost*, about the devastating impact of fast fashion, I knew I had to change my shopping habits. I made a pledge then and there to never buy from a fast-fashion brand again.

That was over two years ago. Since then I have gone one step further and haven't bought anything new, except for underwear, socks and swimwear. Not only have I saved money buying second-hand, but people have complimented me on how I look *more* stylish. Streamlining my wardrobe has allowed me to become my own closet curator and everyday stylist, it has allowed me to mix and match pieces easily and has prevented decision fatigue when deciding what to wear. By streamlining my wardrobe, I not only save the planet's resources, I also gain a wardrobe that reflects my values. All of this, and my passion for fashion hasn't been compromised.

# STREAMLINING YOUR WARDROBE

1. Start with a decluttered wardrobe (see Day 7). Every item of clothing should have a home. Make sure you return it to its home once you've finished using it.

2. Create an inspiration board of your favourite looks. I like using Pinterest, but there are other apps and websites you can check out. You could also get a big piece of paper and stick images you cut out on it. Make sure the board reflects your *actual* life, not your dream life.

3. Examine the inspiration board, reflect on your chosen styles. Are they monochrome looks or do you like pops of colour? Do you prefer a beachy look, or are you more a smart-casual person? Pull out the similar themes to help you decide the best styles for you going forward.

4. Become your own stylist! Style the different items in your wardrobe according to your inspiration board. You can mix and match items however you want! Once again, this is 'creativity within confines' in action – not only will you become more inspired, I guarantee you people will compliment you on your originality.

5. Stick to the shopping ban. Now that you know how much you have in your wardrobe, it's time to be more mindful about your purchases. Continue your shopping ban for the rest of the month (and beyond, if you can) and only buy things you truly need. My motto is 'buy less, but buy better'.

# TIPS FOR SHOPPING YOUR WARDROBE

- After your initial shopping ban, I suggest setting another ban at least once a year. Doing this helps me keep my consumerist tendencies in check!

- Check out minimalist wardrobe ideas, such as developing a Capsule Wardrobe or Project 333.

- Photograph your outfits for one month. You'll be surprised how many different looks you can generate with the items you already have.

- Make yourself accountable. Share your shopping ban with a friend or co-worker, or go through your wardrobe with a stylish friend.

- Apply the 'one-in, one-out' rule: if you want something new, you'll need to donate an older item.

- Write down all your purchases for three to six months. It'll be a shock to see how much you *actually* spend on clothing and accessories.

- Value your money. How you spend your money is a reflection of your values. Let's not put money towards fast-fashion labels, which place profits over the planet and its people.

# DAY 14

# MAKE SECOND-HAND YOUR FIRST CHOICE

There is a lot of debate about the most 'ethical' way of dealing with consumption. I've found that the most cost-effective and eco-friendly thing to do is to buy second-hand because it promotes the use of goods that are already in circulation — no new resources are required, encouraging a more zero waste economy.

When you've completed your shopping ban and thoroughly shopped your wardrobe, you may need to buy some items. Make a list of things you need, not just a list of things you want. This could be more glass jars, a stainless-steel water bottle, a good quality jacket — whatever it is, write it down and search for it second-hand.

I frequent op shops (or thrift stores, as they are called in the United States) as my first shopping destination. You'll be amazed by the quality of items inside. We live in a highly consumerist culture; people are discarding items at a rate that we have never seen before. As recent as the 1990s, there were only four seasons in a year in which clothing stores brought out new styles. But since the rise of fast fashion, stores now have new items weekly. Charity stores are also overwhelmed with the influx of cheap clothing. Often they select the best quality items to sell and the rest are shipped to developing countries for bulk resale, made into industrial rags or sent to landfill.

Homewares is another industry that has recently become part of the fast-fashion industry. The rise of cheap homewares has seen us buying new items constantly, so that even our homes are 'on trend'. It's a sad state of affairs when you see cheap furniture in landfill, not because it's no longer functional, but because it's no longer fashionable.

# MY DECISION-MAKING SHOPPING FLOW CHART!

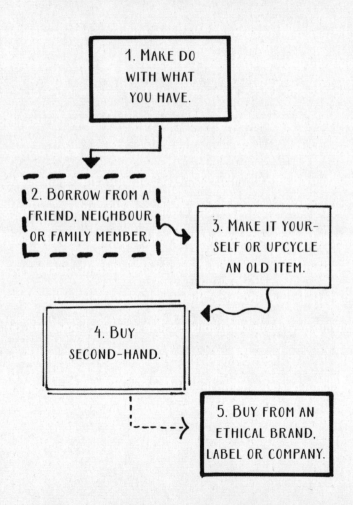

1. MAKE DO WITH WHAT YOU HAVE.

2. BORROW FROM A FRIEND, NEIGHBOUR OR FAMILY MEMBER.

3. MAKE IT YOUR-SELF OR UPCYCLE AN OLD ITEM.

4. BUY SECOND-HAND.

5. BUY FROM AN ETHICAL BRAND, LABEL OR COMPANY.

# TIPS FOR SECOND-HAND SHOPPING

- Try online second-hand stores such as eBay, Craigslist, Gumtree and other consignment/resell websites and apps. When completing your purchase, ask the seller if they can do plastic-free packaging.

- Check out your local markets — there are so many bargains to be had. Bring cash and don't forget to haggle!

- Buy quality over quantity. Look for natural materials such as cotton, linen, silk and wool. Avoid polyester or other synthetic materials. One of the most common micropollutants in our waterways is synthetic fibres from our washing machines.

# DAY 15

# DECLUTTER YOUR HOME
# PART II

This time, we are tackling another major hurdle — letting go of excess stuff from our homes. My story of *stuff* began when I was very little. I always loved collecting things. I couldn't have just one Enid Blyton book or Barbie, I had to collect the whole series. My attachment to *stuff* is reflective of our wider materialistic culture — we feel like we need more things in order to feel secure.

It's hard to break the cycle of buy, accumulate, store. I still have trouble now. Our attachment to material objects affects more than just our physical environment, it reflects our 'inner environment' as well.

Decluttering is the beginning of a journey that allows your home to reflect your lifestyle and values. I reached breaking point when the cost of my consumption had become too high for me; it was affecting my finances and my emotional wellbeing. We surround ourselves with chores, errands and tasks associated with the accumulation and maintenance of our *stuff*, and as a result we have no time to explore the depths of our souls. Isn't that scary?

Today I want to walk you through a simple process for decluttering your home, letting go of your stuff and finally giving yourself the freedom to explore your hearts and minds. It may take longer than a day. In fact, it might take a lifetime, but it is the start of something new. It's a day to embrace less in order to gain more.

# THREE STEPS TO ZERO CLUTTER

**1. REDUCED CLUTTER** This step focuses on *action*; it requires you to go through your home and curate your items to suit your life.

- EXAMINE YOUR HOME Look at all the space you have to work with. The one misconception that people have when it comes to home decluttering is that we believe we don't have enough smart storage solutions. In reality, our homes have more than enough storage – we just have too much stuff! Let the space determine the amount of things you can own. For instance, the size of your cupboard determines the amount of crockery it can hold. The size of the shelf determines how many items it can store. Apply your spending ban rule here.

- MAKE YOUR WAY THROUGH YOUR HOME Go room by room, grouping all the items in each room by type. I have ordered the rooms in accordance with what I believe will have the least to most sentimental items. This allows you to work up towards the items that are hardest to let go.

- KITCHEN
- BATHROOM
- STUDY
- LIVING ROOMS
- BEDROOMS

Find items of the same type and sort them into four piles:

- KEEP
- REPAIR
- SELL/DONATE
- DISPOSE

Now it's time to remove the items from your home (please see Day 26 – dispose of items mindfully). Take photos of the items you are selling and upload them to your chosen website or app. If you are repairing the items, do it immediately! Procrastination leads to the inevitable build-up of more clutter.

2. LOW CLUTTER This step involves *maintenance* and ensuring your home does not get 'clutter creep' (when mysterious clutter creeps into your home without rhyme or reason).

- EVERYTHING MUST HAVE A HOME This is the cardinal rule for keeping your home clutter-free. That's why, once you've decluttered, your space should dictate the amount of stuff you have, not the other way around. Only buy something new when you have a home for it, or if it replaces something you already have (the same tips for shopping your wardrobe in Day 13).

## 3. ZERO CLUTTER This final step is to say *no* to clutter before it enters your home.

- SAYING NO You've already become more discerning about the stuff in your life. By curating your home, you're also curating your life. Does the goodie bag from a work conference fit in with your life's aesthetic? If the answer is no, why not kindly refuse it? Does the gift-with-purchase really suit your needs? If no, why not decline the offer? Saying no is hard for many of us. We live in a society that places security and status on more, not less. I was raised in a household that never said no to anything free. My parents grew up in communist China, so when they moved to Australia and were surrounded by abundance, they clung to it! They were the 'just-in-case' types who said yes to everything, because they always thought that there would be an occasion to use it. I challenge you to start saying no to excess stuff.

# THE NOAH'S ARK RULE TO DECLUTTERING

I created the Noah's Ark rule for all my household items, where the maximum amount of any same item I own is two. It worked for Noah and his ark and it'll work for you! It's the perfect number for household items, such as kitchen utensils, where one can be in the wash, and the other can be in use. No more, no less.

I actually apply the Noah's Ark rule to all individual-use items including towels, bedding, cups and plates. e.g. Noah's Ark rule for towels = two × no. of people in household. So if there are four people, we have a maximum of eight towels.

Of course, you can adapt the Noah's Ark rule to suit your specific needs. It's just a general rule of thumb to ensure I maintain a minimalist lifestyle while balancing the practical realities of everyday life.

# THE GOLDILOCKS METHOD

Apply the Goldilocks method when assessing how much you need. Not too little, not too much, just the right amount. You are the best person to decide how much stuff you need. By having 'just the right amount', you are saying no to wasting Earth's resources, you are saying no to excess clutter in your life, and you are finally saying yes to life.

# REFLECT & REVIEW

---

## DAYS

### 16 – 30

# DAY 16

# GIVE YOURSELF A GREEN PRESCRIPTION

---

We've reached the halfway mark, so now is a good time to explore the great outdoors and remind yourself why we need to lead a zero waste life.

I remember the commute to my nine-to-five job being the hardest part of the day. I lived only a 30-minute walk from work, but chose to drive instead, with the justification that I was wearing heels and didn't want to work up a sweat before the day began. I worked the hours of sunlight, sometimes going to the office before sunrise and leaving as the sun set. There were no windows in this office environment, I mostly ate at my desk and sat in air-conditioned meeting rooms. I was so out of touch with nature, I often forgot what season it was. I didn't see sunshine during a work day for over seven years.

Many of us who live and work in cities experience the same disconnect from nature and it's causing us harm. It's no wonder we don't know where our food comes from, what produce is in season, or what type of trees we pass every day. We are part of the animal kingdom, no matter how far we have removed ourselves from it. Our connection to nature is instinctual and *necessary*.

The best gift I have given myself throughout my zero waste journey is my new-found relationship with the outdoors. I feel most at ease when I am hiking in the bushlands of Australia or the Redwoods of California. Today I challenge you to go outside, take off your shoes, feel the grass between your feet and get your hands dirty. That is real. Not the plastic credit card in your wallet, not the new pair of shoes you've been craving, not the shiny car in your neighbour's garage that you've been eyeing. The soil with which we grow our food, the water that we drink, the air we breathe, the animals and plants in our ecosystem — that is real.

Without all of this, nothing else matters.

# TIPS ON HOW TO
# GET OUTDOORS
# MORE OFTEN

1. EAT LUNCH OUTSIDE Make this a rule. Find a park or a patch of grass and soak up the vitamin D. Take off your shoes if you're feeling rebellious and take time to nourish yourself with good food and fresh air.

2. WALK TO WORK Carry some sensible (yet stylish) shoes in your bag and walk to and from work — it doesn't have to be all the way! Why not get off a few stops earlier on your bus trip and walk the remaining distance? Search for a new work route that involves more parks and greenery.

3. BRING THE OUTDOORS INDOORS It's no secret that I have embraced plant parenthood. I own countless indoor plants that bring greenery into my home. Choose plants that are foolproof to begin with (I suggest Devil's Ivy) and learn to nurture something and watch it grow.

4. SPEND THE WEEKENDS OUTDOORS I try to visit a national park, garden, or beach at least once a week. Most of us live a fair distance from a beautiful nature reserve, so it's all about taking advantage of our weekends to explore the great outdoors.

5. REPLACE OLD HABITS WITH OUTDOOR HABITS Instead of going shopping on a Saturday afternoon, go for a hike with a friend instead. I've also embraced being a tourist in my home town, checking out places I haven't been to before. What new outdoor activities could you take up to replace old habits?

# DAY 17

# BUY *REAL* FOOD

---

During my zero waste journey I've learnt to appreciate where
my food comes from. Look at your dinner plate tonight and ask
yourself: how did the food get from the farm to your plate? How
was it grown? How was it harvested?

When I was about ten years old, my dad brought home a tray
of mangoes. They were a real summer treat for us and that year
there was an extra special guest hidden underneath a ripe mango –
a green tree frog. This was the first time that I realised my food had
a home before it came to me, that it was grown and nurtured before
it arrived on my plate. The mangoes had come from Queensland
and the green tree frog had survived that entire journey.

This no longer happens. While I am a huge believer in food
hygiene, I do question how industrialised and commercialised our

food system has become. We spray our food with pesticides to ward off bugs and to yield us perfect-looking fruits and vegetables. If they are deemed 'imperfect' they are sent to landfill. When did we become a society that throws away perfectly edible food because of a minor blemish?

Real food is imperfect. Mother Nature didn't grow food to look good on display in supermarkets, she created an abundance of food to nurture and nourish us. In our quest for human perfection, we have come to expect the same of our food. Nobody is perfect, why should we expect that of our food?

## THE LOUIS VUITTON PARADOX

Let's talk about the cost of organic produce. I always find it surprising when people can afford to buy a new handbag, yet they refuse to spend extra money on fresh, organic produce. I eat organic food on a student budget because I make it a priority. Buying the best quality you can afford applies to food as much as it does to fashion. Food is medicine and fuel for your body – invest in your long-term health, not in another handbag!

# THREE ZERO WASTE STEPS TO BUYING REAL FOOD

## 1. REDUCED FAKE-FOOD DIET

- BUY PACKAGE-FREE FOOD Most real food doesn't need packaging. Oranges have peels, zucchinis have skin – these items don't need packaging because they already have their own!

- BUY THE 'UGLIES' Choose the wonky cucumber, the lonely banana, the smaller lemon. These are the ones that will most likely go to landfill because of their imperfections. If you choose the uglies, they won't go to waste!

## 2. LOW FAKE-FOOD DIET

- BUY FROM YOUR LOCAL FARMERS Meet the growers of your food and develop relationships with your farmers (see Day 8). It's time to know where your food comes from.

- BUY ORGANIC FOOD, STARTING WITH THE 'DIRTY DOZEN' The 'dirty dozen' are the food items that are most heavily sprayed with pesticides. You should try to buy these organic when possible – it's a great entry point to transitioning to a totally organic diet. I aim to buy organic when it comes to things that grow on vines (berries, grapes, tomatoes) and low to the ground (celery, kale, spinach).

## THE DIRTY DOZEN

1. APPLES
2. STRAWBERRIES
3. GRAPES
4. CELERY
5. PEACHES/NECTARINES
6. SPINACH
7. CAPSICUM/CHILLIES
8. CUCUMBERS
9. POTATOES
10. TOMATOES
11. KALE
12. CHERRIES

## 3. ZERO FAKE-FOOD DIET

- **BUY ONLY ORGANIC PRODUCE** I buy all my produce from organic farmers because firstly, it tastes better and secondly, it reduces the amount of toxic chemicals leeching into the soil.

  I choose an organic delivery service that allows me to return the boxes (totally zero waste) and they select the best produce for me each week. I receive in-season produce at a discounted rate (because I am not buying pineapples in winter, which carry travel expenses), and this allows me to be more creative with my diet. I get to try new fruit and vegetables I previously didn't know existed.

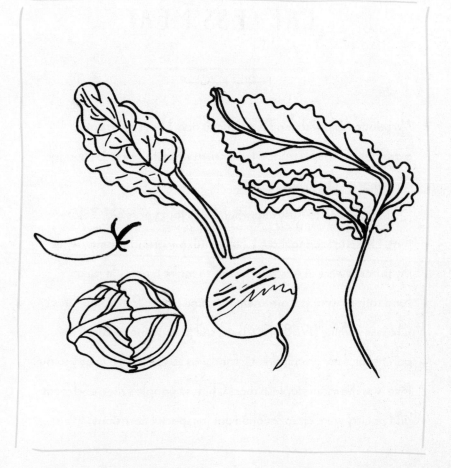

# DAY 18

# EAT LESS MEAT

———————

My relationship with food is a difficult one. I have seen both extremes of the spectrum — I've known what it's like to be hungry, and what it's like to have excess.

I immigrated to Australia when I was four years old. Before that, I lived in Guangzhou, China, with my grandparents, while my parents were in Australia trying to make a new life for us. Food rations were still prevalent in China in the 1980s, the Great Chinese Famine (1958–1961) was still fresh in the minds of my parents and my grandparents. Food was (and still is) a luxury to me. Rice was the main staple in most Chinese people's diet, and meat and poultry were often rationed out for special occasions.

Today, living in Australia, diet labels have become the new religion. We hear all the time about people who are gluten-free, sugar-free, vegetarian or vegan. People are so militant about their approach to food. I don't know about you, but I'm exhausted by it all.

Food to me is a privilege. It is more than just a diet craze; it is the foundation of human functioning. Studying medicine, I see how prevalent eating disorders are and how it's affecting young people. I am always reluctant to put labels on eating and food, because eating is the most basic instinct we have, and we shouldn't place so many rules around it.

# LET'S TALK ABOUT REDUCTIONISM

There is no doubt that eating meat, poultry, fish and dairy has a huge environmental impact on the planet. We live in a world of seven billion people and the livestock used for our meat consumption is one of the major sources of greenhouse gas emissions. If I were to encourage any label for your diet, I would suggest 'reductionism' – simply put, this just means eating less meat.

## TIPS ON HOW TO REDUCE YOUR MEAT CONSUMPTION

1. **MEATLESS MONDAYS** Start with one day in which you don't consume meat. It doesn't have to be a Monday or even a full day – it could even be simply avoiding meat for breakfast for a whole month. Whatever you choose, aim for a gentle initial goal to reduce your meat intake. Think of the cumulative difference this makes over a lifetime!

2. **REPLACE RATHER THAN REFUSE** Instead of seeing meatless meals as a form of deprivation, see it as an opportunity to replace meat with different options. Creativity within confines – by saying no to meat, you are saying yes to different plant-based foods! There

are so many vegetarian and vegan recipes out there. Trust me, if you don't tell people it's vegetarian, most people won't even notice.

3. **EAT THE COLOURS OF THE RAINBOW** Make your meals sexy by including foods of all colours of the rainbow, and you won't even notice that there isn't any meat on your plate.

4. **EAT MORE AND WORRY LESS** As part of the zero waste paradox, the more package-free produce you eat, the less you'll worry about your weight. I eat more now than I ever have, my plate is always full and I never feel like I'm missing out. I definitely don't count calories and I've lost weight as a result!

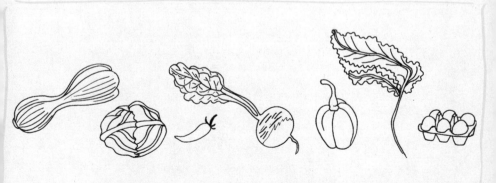

# DAY 19

# LEARN TO EMBRACE MINIMALISM

During 2014, my husband and I lived in my in-laws' home for a year. This was when I quit my job and was at a loss of what to do with my life. They had moved overseas and kindly offered us their four-bedroom home to live in so that we could save money. We relocated from the inner suburbs of Sydney to perfect suburbia.

I had so much space, and boy, was I on a mission to fill it! I bought storage solutions for my shoes and clothing, shelves to organise my kitchen goods, and more empty containers to store all my things in! I was living the Great Australian Dream – literally, in a huge house with a white picket fence – yet I was the unhappiest I had ever been in my life.

You see, the Great Australian Dream wasn't *my* dream.

I missed being back in the heart of the city where I didn't have to drive everywhere, I missed being close to the water, close to my friends and, most of all, I missed the energy that living in the city gave me.

After a year, we moved back to my small apartment in Sydney.

I had less space than ever, but it was here I was happiest.

Downsizing from a four-bedroom home to a 59-square metre apartment meant I had to embrace minimalism. My definition of minimalism is simple — live with less stuff so that you can live *more*.

There are no set rules on how much stuff you must have in order to be a minimalist, you define what your version of *less* is.

# THREE STEPS TO A MORE MINIMALIST LIFE

## 1. REDUCED STUFF

A. **GET RID OF YOUR CDs AND DVDs** Subscription services such as Spotify and Netflix mean that we don't need hard copies of movies and music anymore. Go through your collection and donate items that are available online.

B. **LIVE A PAPERLESS LIFE** An easy way to live a paperless life is to download a scanner app for your smartphone. There are apps that use your phone camera to take pictures of your paperwork and convert them into PDFs, which you can then save to an online storage system. The only items you need hard copies of are official documents, such as birth and marriage certificates.

## 2. LOW STUFF

A. **GO DIGITAL** Scan your photos and store them on a hard drive or a cloud storage system. That way you can access them anywhere, anytime and you'll have no old photo albums to store!

B. **BORROW BOOKS OR USE AN E-READER** For those of us who like the feel and smell of books, try borrowing them from the library before you consider purchasing them. I use an e-reader and have a Kindle unlimited subscription so I can access books electronically whenever I travel.

## 3. ZERO STUFF

A. **GO CAR-LESS** I haven't owned a car for years! I walk everywhere, use public transport or Uber, or hire a car when necessary. It's saved me so much money. Assess your life and see if you can live without a car, or even just reduce the number of cars in the household.

B. **JOIN A 'TOOL LIBRARY'** How often do you actually use your electric drill? Or your ladder? Do an internet search and see if there is a community centre that lends out these items or if there is a 'tool library' near you. Before you buy new, why not consider borrowing from a neighbour or friend or even paying someone to lend these items to you for a day? This applies to most things you don't use every day, such as gym equipment and electronics.

# DAY 20

# SPREAD THE WORD

―――――――――
―――――――――

Living a zero waste life can feel like a lonely journey, especially at the beginning. But today is the day to find like-minded people and share your experiences.

My journey started with Instagram. I took my first photo in a dimly lit kitchen to celebrate replacing my old plastic containers with glass ones. Since then, I've gained tens of thousands of followers and share daily tips about zero waste living with people from all around the world. The community I've gained has enabled me to write this book and also allowed me to establish long lasting friendships with kindred spirits.

A key tip to sharing your new ideas with others is to be *kind*. Be kind to yourself, perfection is not the goal. Be kind to others, even if they don't share your views. If your family or friends ask about your plastic-free diet, share it with them, but don't sit on your high horse about any of your new-found values.

# FIVE WAYS TO SPREAD THE WORD ABOUT ZERO WASTE LIVING

**1. GET ON THE SOCIALS** Check out Instagram, Facebook and online blogs to find and share ideas and discover new friends!

**2. ORGANISE A DOCUMENTARY NIGHT** I love entertaining guests and often have people over to watch a documentary about social or environmental issues. We discuss the film afterwards and the conversations that generally follow are some of the most insightful conversations I've ever had with my friends.

**3. ORGANISE A PLASTIC-FREE EVENT** I helped set up a Clean-Up Australia day for my medical school, and it was so much fun! Maybe you can organise a plastic-free morning tea, or a free viewing of a documentary for your local community.

**4. EDUCATE YOURSELF** I often find myself lost in the vortex of the internet, when I could be using my time more wisely. Why not change your habits from scrolling to studying and learning more about things that matter, like environmentalism, politics, health and other important issues?

**5. HELP OUT A FRIEND** Organise a decluttering session with a friend. After you have decluttered your own home (see Days 7 and 15), your friends and family will be amazed by the transformation, and requests for your help will come far and wide. Take it as a compliment and help out others where you can. Warning – decluttering is addictive!

# DAY 21

# DECLUTTER YOUR MIND

---

Mental decluttering is just as important as physical decluttering. This is the final day in the three-day decluttering challenge and is dedicated to freeing the mind and letting go of toxic relationships.

In decluttering my home I stripped away the excess, the layers of stuff we use to hide who we really are. For the first time in my life, my values and beliefs were exposed for the world to see. It was liberating. In doing this I had inadvertently decluttered my relationships as well – I no longer tolerated toxic friendships. But the biggest relationship I changed was the one with myself.

Letting go of physical unwanted baggage also allowed me to let go of mental and emotional baggage. I removed the superfluous and examined what I really wanted to do with my life. When I was younger I always wanted to be an aerospace doctor, studying the effects of space travel on the human body. I was so excited about the prospect of learning about the unknown. But then a teacher had dismissed my goals, making me feel as if I was acting too big for my boots. As I grew older, I always felt like I was lacking at work even though I successfully climbed the corporate ladder. Something was amiss, I felt I wasn't enough. All these moments of loneliness were not because of my external circumstances, but because I wasn't being my true self. A friend of mine introduced me to the saying 'You do you' — a motto I've lived by ever since.

# THREE STEPS TO GETTING RID OF YOUR MENTAL CLUTTER

## 1. REDUCED MENTAL CLUTTER

A.  UNFOLLOW OR HIDE POSTS It's time do a social media clear-out!
Start by unfollowing or hiding posts from people or companies who
irritate or annoy you. Your social media feed should inspire and
connect you with others and be a space for learning. The internet
should be a tool used for purposeful interaction, not a place for
hatred or negativity.

B.  REMOVE ADVERTISEMENTS Remove the 'noise' in your home
by removing labels from objects. Colourful labels with shiny
marketing slogans add to the clutter in a room. One benefit
of living a zero waste life is that you're exposed to a lot less
packaging, and therefore less marketing. Mute the TV when
commercials come on, unsubscribe from email advertising –
the less noise we have, the less marketing we are exposed to,
and the less temptation there is to buy more stuff.

## 2. LOW MENTAL CLUTTER

A.  MAKE SELF-CARE RITUALS Make a 'joy list' of five to ten activities
    that are nourishing to your soul. Whenever you have a stressful
    day or feel overwhelmed, treat yourself to one or more of those
    activities. This may include a bubble bath, a slow morning reading
    the paper, or seeking refuge in your favourite café with a book.

B.  ESTABLISH A MORNING ROUTINE During the first one to two
    hours of the day I like to be in autopilot mode. Decision fatigue is
    something we all face. We can make up to 100 decisions within
    the morning hours, so why not save that energy for things that truly
    matter? I have a written routine for what the first hour of my day
    looks like, and I don't deviate from it. This includes the activities
    that help me 'prime' myself for the day, such as meditation, light
    exercise and eating a healthy breakfast. Setting yourself up for
    the day allows you to be more effective, creative and productive.

# 3. ZERO MENTAL CLUTTER

A. **PRACTISE MEDITATION** This has truly changed my life. Sitting quietly with oneself is hard, yet it is the most rewarding daily habit you can establish. I suggest for beginners to try a short guided meditation using an app. Start with a ten-day meditation commitment and experience the benefits immediately.

B. **BREAK THE TWITCH** How often have we interrupted a conversation to check our phones? Do you reach for your phone whenever you have a quiet moment to yourself? It's time for a digital detox! Start small (I turn my phone on aeroplane mode whenever I'm studying or writing), and eventually you can extend this to having a day offline every week.

C. MAKE SLEEP A PRIORITY Did you know if you have fewer than seven to eight hours of sleep at night, it's the equivalent to being drunk? Fatigue is a huge issue we are facing in the workforce. Our 24/7 connectedness has made it almost impossible for us to disconnect and, as a result, our sleep suffers. Remove electronics from your bedroom and set an old-fashioned alarm clock. Reduce any source of noise and light pollution. Giving yourself a proper night's sleep is the most effective boost to your productivity.

# DAY 22

# MAKE DO AND MEND

———————

———————

'Make do and mend' is a wonderful slogan from World War II that we should all be embracing. Nowadays, sewing is a lost skill and mending clothes can be more expensive than buying something new. However, the financial cost of a clothing item doesn't reflect the cost of the item to the planet. Fashion is the second most polluting industry on the planet, after fossil fuels. Whenever we throw away a clothing item, we are also throwing away the precious resources used to make it. It's time to respect our resources and repair the clothing we have.

The 'make do and mend' attitude doesn't only apply to clothing, the same goes with all the products in our life, in particular, electronics. Have you noticed how the electronics of your grandparents' or parents' era lasted for decades? Planned obsolescence is now ingrained in design processes and electronics have a turnover period almost as fast as our fashion cycle.

When I was younger, my dad was a jack-of-all-trades who knew how to fix anything, mend clothing and even cut hair. He learnt everything on his own (without YouTube), because we didn't have the extra money to be fleeting with our purchases. I've come around to applying the same rule now. I prefer to buy the best quality I can afford and repair the goods when I need to, rather than replacing them with another cheap item as soon as they break. Looking back, I can see that my parents have been the best sources of inspiration to live an eco-friendly life.

# THREE WAYS TO EMBRACE THE MAKE DO AND MEND ATTITUDE

**1. FIND A TAILOR** Having your clothes and second-hand finds tailored can give them a modern look and is a great way to upcycle old pieces and give them new life.

**2. LEARN BASIC SEWING SKILLS** Even if you've never picked up a needle and thread before, there is no excuse not to learn. Sewing is so accessible now, you can watch a video on YouTube, or even better, get a family member or friend to teach you!

**3. ATTEND COMMUNITY WORKSHOPS** Look up local community groups and check out the free workshops available. There are workshops on bike maintenance, woodworking and cooking – there is so much we can learn!

# FAST FASHION FACTS
# TO GIVE YOU A
# KICK UP THE BUM

## Did you know?

1. It takes 2720 litres of water to make a t-shirt – that's how much one person would normally drink over a 3 year period!

2. 95% of discarded clothing can be recycled or upcycled.

3. A garment is worn just four times on average.

4. Only about 15 per cent of donated clothing is actually sold again locally in opportunity shops.

5. The world now consumes a staggering 80 billion pieces of clothing each year. This is up 400% on two decades ago.

# PARTICIPATING IN THE SHARE ECONOMY

Much as we have subscriptions services for our music and books, we can also use services to hire and rent clothing. Special occasion clothing, like cocktail dresses, are usually only worn once and never taken out of your closet again. Why not hire a dress for the night and save yourself some money and wardrobe space?

# DAY 23

# VALUE EXPERIENCES
# OVER STUFF

---

I attended a funeral of a family friend named Harry, who died
at the ripe old age of 93. He had survived his own hero's journey
through Nazi concentration camps, losing his family in World War
II and immigrating to Australia, leaving everything he knew behind.
My favourite moment of the ceremony was when a friend of Harry's
raised her glass and exclaimed, 'Here's a toast to Harry, who said
to always have champagne in the fridge, because there is always a
reason to celebrate.' The speeches that came after were filled with
stories of loyalty, love and laughter. No one spoke about the brand
of his shoes, the make of his car or even what he did for a living.

In our deaths, we want to be remembered for our character, the
experiences we had and the love we shared, so why do we focus so

much on 'stuff' in our everyday lives? There aren't any marketing campaigns about courage. There isn't a TV advertisement about the care you showed for your elderly mother. There isn't a billboard showing the positive effects of laughter. All around us, we are told that more stuff is what matters.

I now care less about the brands I wear, whether I live in the 'right' suburb and the sort of car I drive. But I care more about purpose-driven work, the love of my husband and the joy of my family and friends. In other words, I care more about what will be said in my eulogy, and less about what's in my resume.

Today is a day to reflect on your own value system. The exercise on the next page will take some time — it might be confronting; it might even be tearful. But at the end of it, you'll have a clearer idea of what truly matters to you.

# WRITE YOUR OWN EULOGY

Take a big breath in and out. Be honest with yourself and write down what you would like to have read out as your eulogy. Here are some questions to get you started:

- Who do you want to be remembered for?

- What makes you happiest?

- What would be your greatest contributions?

- Who do you love the most?

- What key moments have shaped who you are?

Circle the keywords in your eulogy. These are the values you truly
want to be working towards.

# ZERO WASTE TRAVEL

As an aerospace engineer, I have no doubt that the current form
of aviation technology leaves a high carbon footprint, however, here
is how I've come to make peace with it. To me, living a zero waste
life has always been about making sensible and practical switches
and unfortunately, there is currently no sensible switch for air travel.
No available mass transport option uses renewable energies and
travelling long distances by boat is not practical for most people.

Travelling to visit family, for work and to experience the world has
enriched my life beyond belief. I have seen the ice-capped mountains
of Iceland and the Redwoods of California, and it has made me even
more passionate about protecting this planet for the future. Travelling
has educated and humbled me, it's made me appreciate the value of
gaining experiences over stuff.

# THREE TIPS TO REDUCE YOUR WASTE WHEN TRAVELLING

## CARBON OFFSET

Carbon offset is currently the best compromise between air travel and sustainability. Technology has not advanced to a stage where a low carbon option is available for air travel, but if you do your research you can buy carbon offsets from a reliable and reputable company.

## BRING YOUR OWN FOOD

For long flights, email the airline beforehand to let them know you're bringing your own food so they don't have to cater to you. For short flights, just bring your own snack pack and refuse the airline snacks. Don't forget your zero waste kit! Bring your own reusable coffee cup and ask the cabin crew to pour directly into your cup. Remind them that you don't need straws, stirrers, or napkins because you already have your own.

## TRAVEL WITH CARRY-ON LUGGAGE ONLY

Be an easy-breezy, minimalist traveller and fly with only carry-on luggage. You won't feel burdened by your bags and you'll have far less waiting time. This also means less weight on the plane, which means less fuel is required! The key to travelling light is packing clothing items that you can easily mix and match.

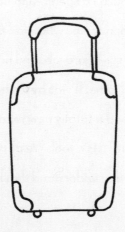

# DAY 24

# VOTE WITH YOUR DOLLAR

———————
———————

I cannot reflect on my zero waste life without talking about what started me on this journey in the first place — money.

I grew up with little money and there never seemed to be enough of it to go around. When I started working and earning a good salary, I wanted to *feel* rich, so I started spending like a Rockefeller! I cared more about how much I'd spend than how much I could save. The sudden loss of money was what had prompted my zero waste journey. I'd quit my six-figure job, and had to learn how to make ends meet on one income. It was by losing that access to easy money that I developed a totally new relationship with it.

Money is not a dirty word; it is a tool. We all need money to survive, but we also need to understand that it is a valuable resource. We are fortunate enough to live in a country where we can exercise our democratic rights every day by voting with our dollar – how we spend our money should align with our values.

We live in a society of fast food, fast fashion and fast relationships – the focus is on quantity rather than quality, speed rather than merit. We need to raise our standards to combat the cheap and convenient. Our money needs to be channelled towards causes that focus on grace, gentleness and longevity.

My relationship with money is now one of respect. Money is a tool used to support our value system. When climate change feels oo big to tackle, or whenever we feel overwhelmed by the state of politics, remember we have the power to vote with our dollar. Let's choose to spend our money wisely.

# THE THREE-STEP METHOD
# TO ZERO MONEY WASTE

## 1. REDUCED MONEY WASTE

A.  QUESTION YOUR PURCHASES Before you buy anything new, consider the hierarchy of spending (see 'My rules for shopping' in Day 14). Ask yourself:

    i.   Do I really need it?

    ii.   Can I borrow it?

    iii.   Can I buy it second-hand?

    iv.   If I really do need to buy it, does the company I'm purchasing from align with my values?

B.  LEARN HOW TO BUDGET This is the most important skill for 'adulting'. If you don't already know how to budget, it's as simple as this: *your spending should be less than your earnings.* Establish a set budget for the following:

1.  Rent/mortgage

2.  Groceries

3.  Transport (including car)

4.  Utilities

5.  Debt payments

6.  Savings

7.  Pocket money

This is in order of priority, one must have a roof over one's head, food in one's belly and a means to get to work before setting aside discretionary money to spend. I use an app to log all my purchases. Do this for one week and you'll be surprised to find where your money goes. Make sure you stay within your budget, apply some discipline and adjust your spending accordingly.

## 2. LOW MONEY WASTE

**SAVE BEFORE YOU SPEND** We all have goals in life, but how many times have we let our bank account dictate our lives, rather than us dictating our bank balance? We need to tell our money where to go, not the other way around. By putting yourself on a regular spending ban and living by minimalist values, you can save enough money to achieve your dreams.

## 3. ZERO MONEY WASTE

**CHANGE YOUR MINDSET** The greatest lesson I learnt on this journey is how I've changed my mindset about money. Respect your money, and it'll respect you. You need to think of money as a renewable resource. You can always make more money, but you can't make more time. How you spend your money is a reflection of your time and energy, so don't waste it.

# ZERO MONEY WASTE — SMALL THINGS ADD UP!

The easiest way to see how the small changes you're making save you and the planet is by doing some simple maths. Take bringing your own lunch to work every day, for instance. Buying lunch out can easily cost $15 a day. $15 × 5 = $75 a week, which equates to $3,750 a year. That's a long-haul plane ticket for two people! The key is to meal prep a couple of days in advance. I also like to cook extra for dinner so I can take leftovers for work the next day. Not only does bringing your lunch save money, it also prevents plastic take-away packaging and excess waste.

# DAY 25

# BE OF SERVICE

---

The day I quit my job, I didn't know what to do with myself. I felt scared by the new-found freedom. Everyone told me to enjoy my 'funemployment', but I couldn't remember the last time I had an empty schedule free from work, chores or errands. What would you do if your life was a blank slate?

I was walking home, pondering that same question, when I passed by my local youth centre. I'd gone by a hundred times before, but it was as if it was the first time I truly saw the children playing in the large hall, the art that was hung in the windows, the graffiti that was sprayed across the brick walls. I had been so caught up in my own busyness that I'd never really thought about the purpose of the centre, and what I could do to help. That was my attitude: I was always too busy to volunteer my time.

I signed up to volunteer at the youth centre the next day, and then I volunteered my Friday nights to mentoring teenagers in my neighbourhood. At first, I thought I was there to provide a service, but instead theses interactions provided a service to me. While giving back, I forgot my troubles and doubts about my career. In helping others I helped myself. That's the power of giving. Through this small act, I realised that I wanted to go back to university to become a doctor. I wanted to dedicate my life to being of service.

I would never have thought about volunteering in the past, but getting out of your own head and helping another human being is a balm for the soul.

# FIVE WAYS YOU CAN BE OF SERVICE TODAY

1. **DONATE YOUR TIME** It can be every week, once a month, or even once a year. Find a cause you're passionate about and volunteer your time. Giving money is great, but there's something even more special about being able to help out directly.

2. **A FRIEND IN NEED** Donate your time to a friend or a family member, for example, with babysitting or decluttering, and don't ask for anything back.

3. **SIGN UP FOR AN EVENT** Find out if there are any local clean-up events or sustainability workshops running nearby and volunteer to participate. Ask your friends and family to join you!

4. **DO THREE RANDOM ACTS OF KINDNESS** This can be anything, ranging from cooking a meal for a neighbour, paying for a stranger's coffee or buying flowers for the local retirement home. These small acts of kindness can brighten someone's day.

**5. SEND OUT GRATITUDE CARDS** When was the last time you received something in the mail? Send a card to let someone know you're thinking of them. Your note doesn't have to serve a purpose, other than to be a reminder that the person who receives it is loved.

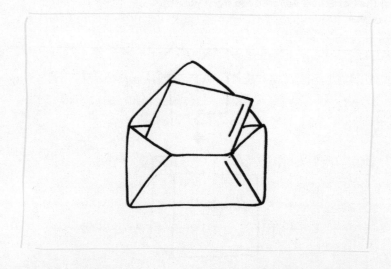

# DAY 26

# DISPOSE OF ITEMS
# MINDFULLY

There is a lot of decluttering advice out there but most books and blogs don't talk about what to do with the items you've cleared out. Today is a day to mindfully upcycle, recycle, donate and dispose of the items you've removed from your life.

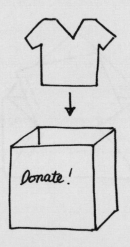

## DONATE

Only donate items that are in good condition. A rule of thumb is to consider whether you yourself would be happy buying them.

POSSIBLE DONATION AVENUES:

- Donate to a women's refuge or homeless shelter
- Donate your old suits and business attire to a 'dress-for-success' charity
- Donate your clothing to a refugee centre
- Donate your clothing to a preschool or school for dress-ups
- Hold a swap meet with your family and friends to exchange clothes
- Hold a swap meet at your school, university or workplace
- Set up a 'Free' box in your workplace or local community for people to pick up donated goods

## SELL

For some of us, the decluttering process will unearth clothes that still have tags on them, or designer pieces that have only been worn once or twice. It's time to make some of that money back!

### QUICK IDEAS FOR SELLING YOUR CLOTHING ITEMS

1. Sell on popular websites or apps such as eBay or Gumtree. You can also try out other selling apps like Carousell and Poshmark, or local buy-and-sell stores on Facebook.

2. Organise a stall with friends at your local markets.

3. Organise a garage sale at home.

4. Sell your items to a consignment store.

## UPCYCLING AND RECYCLING

If donating or selling your items aren't viable options, consider upcycling or recycling your clothing to avoid it becoming landfill.

1. Donate clothing to a rag trade company, which recycles old clothing into rags for industrial use.

2. Cotton t-shirts can be cut up and used for your own cleaning rags (I store mine in a rag basket for easy access and use).

3. Cotton or linen clothing can be cut up and used as napkins. Or get your sewing kit out to make this material into zero waste bags for produce, for example, a nice linen bread bag you can take to the farmers' market.

4. Clothing can be donated to a veterinary clinic or school for animal use.

5. Electronics can be recycled at an e-waste collection site – check your local council for dates and locations.

6. Batteries can be recycled at your local supermarket and electronic stores. Some libraries even have lightbulb, battery and phone recycling collections.

7. Take photos of your items and post them as 'free for collection' on Facebook, Gumtree and other social media sites. As they say, one man's trash is another man's treasure!

## MAKE YOUR OWN CLOTH NAPKINS

Let's talk paper towels and napkins. These single-use items are generally used for less than 10 minutes before they are thrown away to add to landfill. Millions of trees are cut down each year for these disposable items, which are rarely recycled. To break this habit, I collect secondhand napkins, and I also sew my own using upcycled fabric. This is a great way to upcycle old bed sheets, cotton t-shirts and even towels. I've created a napkin and tea towel drawer in my kitchen and they make great presents. Such an easy switch, just use them and wash them — easy!

# CREATE NOT CONSUME

It was a Sunday afternoon, I had just come home with a bag full of clothes after spending a few hours at the local shopping centre. I was sipping my takeaway iced chocolate while checking my Instagram and Facebook feeds. After an hour of mindless scrolling, I sat down for an evening of TV, watching housewives yell at each other. This was a regular Sunday for me. Looking back now, all I can think about are the hours I lost in wasteful consumption – blindly shopping for more stuff, consuming empty calories and indulging in the vortex of social media and televised trash.

We all have to consume to some level, but mindless consumption has been weaved seamlessly into our lives so that we don't even known we are doing it anymore. It's the ultimate form of propaganda.

Instead of spending our time passively consuming, what if we switched those hours to actively creating. How many projects, passions or hobbies have you said no to because you didn't have the time? The truth is, we all have the time, we just don't make our projects a priority. As the meme goes 'You have as many hours in the day as Beyoncé'. We need to transform ourselves from a culture of consumers to creators.

Since I embraced a zero waste lifestyle, I've gained more time. I've had time to start a successful Instagram account, to volunteer, to write this book and to study full-time. Most importantly, I've gained more time to laugh and love. What would you do if you had more time?

# MAP OUT YOUR TIME

1. Allow yourself 15–30 minutes to do this activity. Take a big breath in and out. Be honest with yourself and write down all the activities you have completed in the last week, broken up into hourly blocks. (Break it down into half hour blocks if you need to.)

| Monday | Tuesday | Wednesday | Thursday | Friday | Saturday | Sunday |
|--------|---------|-----------|----------|--------|----------|--------|
|        |         |           |          |        |          |        |
|        |         |           |          |        |          |        |
|        |         |           |          |        |          |        |
|        |         |           |          |        |          |        |
|        |         |           |          |        |          |        |
|        |         |           |          |        |          |        |
|        |         |           |          |        |          |        |
|        |         |           |          |        |          |        |
|        |         |           |          |        |          |        |

2. Using a highlighter, mark all the times you were mindlessly consuming. These include activities without a purpose such as:

- Watching television

- Scrolling through social media

- Mindlessly surfing the internet

- Shopping because you were bored

- Eating because you were bored

3. Tally up these hours for the week. Multiply it by 52. This is the number of 'lost hours' per year.

**4.** Now write a list of all the things you've always wanted to do. Be honest, be bold, be adventurous.

5. Compare that list to your lost hours. You've now found the time to do these things! Replace your mindless consumption with the activities on your new list – you can plan ahead here.

| Monday | Tuesday | Wednesday | Thursday | Friday | Saturday | Sunday |
|--------|---------|-----------|----------|--------|----------|--------|
|        |         |           |          |        |          |        |
|        |         |           |          |        |          |        |
|        |         |           |          |        |          |        |
|        |         |           |          |        |          |        |
|        |         |           |          |        |          |        |
|        |         |           |          |        |          |        |
|        |         |           |          |        |          |        |
|        |         |           |          |        |          |        |
|        |         |           |          |        |          |        |

# DAY 28

# MAINTAINING MINIMALISM

---

---

I've always had 'magpie' tendencies, the need to accumulate shiny stuff to nest in and feel secure, but embracing minimalism has allowed me to appreciate the art of less (see Day 19). By stripping away the layers of stuff that surrounded me, I peeled back the layers of guilt, doubt and fear. We surround ourselves with physical stuff so we don't have to deal with the mental and emotional stuff, the *hard stuff*. In taking everything away, I had to tackle the hard stuff, the questions that leave you cold at night, the fears that leave you breathless, the emotional baggage that has kept you stagnant. Minimalism has forced me to confront my most vulnerable self, and for that I am grateful.

Applying the principles of minimalism has given me the gift of gratitude — I see the beauty in the everyday. I delight in the first crunch of a good piece of sourdough toast, the smell of eucalyptus in my street, the sight of soft peach-coloured light filtering through my windows at sunrise. Like zero waste living, life's precious moments are about small but significant steps that make a big cumulative difference. Railing against excess has allowed me to make room for deeper introspection. Less stuff has given me more time. Less waste has given me more space. I have finally gained my identity back.

Today is a day to slow down and appreciate the art of having less, a day in which you ask yourself what matters in your life.

# FIVE WAYS TO MAINTAIN
# A MINIMALIST LIFE

**1. HAVE A DONATION BOX READY** I have a foldable grocery bag by the front door that I use to store items I no longer want. Having a bag or box ready for donation is a nice way to maintain a decluttered home. Whenever the container gets full, just grab it and take it to the local charity shop. It also serves as a visual reminder to not buy any more than you need.

**2. DO A TEN-MINUTE CLEAN-UP** I hate waking up to an untidy house. Your home should be your sanctuary, and a 'noisy' home filled with clutter will not give you the recuperation that you need. So, before I go to sleep, I set a timer to do a quick tidy-up to return everything to its home. Setting a timer allows you to limit yourself and makes it feel like a game!

**3. DO A REGULAR SPRING CLEAN** At the beginning of every season, go through your home and do another three-day decluttering session. It's amazing to see the clutter that can creep into your house!

**4. GET YOUR FAMILY INVOLVED** Do not get rid of other people's stuff for them – instead, lead by example and gently guide them into a life of less. Engage them in conversations about why you're choosing to live a minimalist life. Educate, don't mandate!

**5. JUST SAY NO!** The easiest way to maintain a minimalist life is to prevent items from coming into your home in the first place. Don't let your stuff consume you!

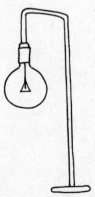

# DAY 29

# GET INVOLVED!

---

I am the first to admit that in the past I never thought too much about environmental politics. Sure, I cared about climate change, air pollution and endangered species, but these problems had always seemed too daunting and too hard to tackle. I think we all feel that same sense of being overwhelmed, that the problems of the world are too big for lil' old me, surely, someone else will take care of it. The problem is, if everyone in the world thought like that, there would be no one to take care of it.

I am grateful to live in Australia, where the air is clean and the water is drinkable. I remember going back to China after living in Australia for a while and walking through old neighbourhoods where I grew up. The lush edible flowers in my uncle's street were gone, the river in which my father swam had been replaced by a tarry stream, and the blue skies were hidden by a persistent smog. In less than a decade, China had become unrecognisable. All in the name of progress.

Clean water, clean air, clean soil is the birth right of all living beings. When people ask me, 'What is the hardest part of living a zero waste life?' I always say the same thing – it's that I can no longer be ignorant of the state of our planet.

Engaging in active citizenry is about gaining our power back. Caring about the world means taking positive action to make positive changes. Today is a day to get involved.

# THE
# RIPPLE
# EFFECT

A university tutor once said to me, 'I'm happy to just be a general practitioner; I don't need to shake the boat and make huge waves of change in medicine'. I thought about how wrong she was, because she had, in fact, encouraged a profound wave of change in me. In her own humble way, she taught me compassion and the importance of standing firm in your beliefs. That is the power of the ripple effect, whereby your daily actions have the power to influence others. What seems like a small drop in the ocean, such as saying no to a plastic bag, has the power to create ripples of change across the tidepools of life.

Your individual action can encourage others to do the same. Through leading by example, your influence can be profound. Don't forget your sphere of influence when you think that your actions are too small to count. You never know what ripple effect they may have towards the greater good.

# FIVE WAYS TO GET INVOLVED

**1. BECOME A LETTER WRITER** I never believed in letter writing or voicing my opinion before I started my zero waste journey, but I now realise that if we want change, we have to create it ourselves. I emailed my organic box delivery service about their sudden increase in plastic use. They responded and listened to my suggestions about going plastic-free and it worked! My organic delivery box now comes with no plastic! This was a reminder to me that small individual actions can make a huge difference.

**2. EDUCATE YOURSELF** Find out who your local member of parliament is, visit their website and understand their policies. If you're not happy about something, give them a call or send them an email. Watch quality news media, read longform investigative articles, educate yourself on issues that you're passionate about – and then do something about it!

### 3. ENGAGE IN ACTIVE CITIZENRY Actions speak louder than words. Instead of complaining about the problem, do something about it, even if it's something small. Go for a beach clean-up, volunteer in a tree-planting activity, set up a recycling station at a community event. Whatever it is, do something tangible to reflect your values.

### 4. PARTICIPATE IN MARCHES AND RALLIES Don't be afraid to participate in non-violent protests. In 2016, I joined my first People's Climate March, where thousands of people rallied on the Sydney streets to show solidarity in the fight against climate change. I was inspired, humbled and utterly grateful to be part of a group of people who cared so much about the health of the environment.

### 5. BE A POSITIVE INFLUENCE ON THE WORLD Lead by example, don't preach, stay humble. That's the best way to promote change.

# DAY 30

# REST AND REVIEW

---

Resting is underrated in our society. Our work successes are measured by productivity goals, efficiency targets and units of output, but no one measures rest and recuperation. Rest, sleep and relaxation are completely necessary for our mental and physical wellbeing. We can't take care of others if we don't take of ourselves.

I am a typical Type-A personality, with a competitive streak from my dad and a strong work ethic that I inherited from my mum. I wouldn't know how to rest, even if I tried. Yet over the course of my zero waste journey, I've learned to slow down, appreciate the beauty of the motto 'less is more' and how to rest.

DAYS

REST AND REWARD

Today is the final day of the thirty-day challenge. A chance to rest and review what you have achieved, to see how far you've come and to feel empowered. Today we accept that zero waste is a goal, not a number, and that our aim is to continue doing small but significant things to improve as we follow our zero waste journey.

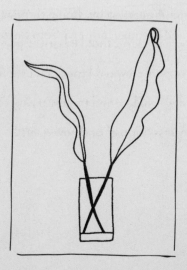

# BECOME A ZERO WASTE ENGINEER

Write down all the challenges and issues you have faced this month when trying to live a zero waste life. Was it grocery shopping? Letting go of stuff you didn't need? Getting your partner involved?

Examine these problems, one by one. I want you to turn each problem upside down and design a solution to it. Let's reverse engineer a solution to the problem! Remember, this is all about getting your creativity flowing! That's the key to living a zero waste life – instead of thinking it's an overwhelming task, solve the problem by designing a solution. Brainstorm with your family and friends and become your own zero waste engineer!

| Problem | Zero Waste Solution |
|---|---|
|  |  |
|  |  |
|  |  |
|  |  |
|  |  |
|  |  |
|  |  |
|  |  |
|  |  |
|  |  |
|  |  |
|  |  |

# CONCLUSION

We live in a society that talks trash, thinks relationships are disposable and treats the planet like garbage. We use our most valuable resources, the basic units of life – earth, water and air – as if they are in limitless supply. We dump our rubbish on the planet as if there is endless space for landfill. It's time to say no. We can all start by just saying no.

I hope the past thirty days have shown you that environmentalism isn't about overwhelming pollution statistics or scary climate change scenarios. It's about embracing simple, everyday switches, and being an everyday activist.

Living a zero waste life has allowed me to let go of old habits so that I can live an authentic life – one that is in alignment with my values. It has given me a new lease on life that has far exceeded all expectations: I am now back at university studying to become a doctor, writing a book, travelling the world with my husband, and none of this could have happened if I didn't change my habits. I hope you have experienced the same joy I have in making these changes. Your journey doesn't have to be as drastic, but I do hope it is as dramatic. During my zero waste journey, I have undergone a transformation far deeper than a plastic-free diet. I have changed into a person who respects the planet's resources, as well as my own. Plastic is Mother Nature's non-renewable resource, and time is ours. Neither should be wasted.

Zero waste living relies on individual actions making a cumulative difference. We think that saying no to one plastic bottle doesn't matter, but what if 7 billion of us said no? Zero waste is the goal but your lifestyle doesn't have to be perfect to make a big difference. We don't always have to get it right, but we can always improve.

I started this journey focused on being *independent*. I wanted to be financially independent, trying to make ends meet on one income, and to live a life that was independent of lack-lustre work. But through this journey I've not only gained my independence, I've come to understand that we are all *interdependent*. All our actions are interrelated, interconnected, intertwined. We are all dependent on one another. We need to work together, to combine our skills and talents if we are to continue to *thrive* on this planet. Not just *survive*, but thrive.

Before my 'broken dam fiasco of 2014', I followed a path of least resistance. In accepting that path, I had chosen a life that was on autopilot. In removing the plastic from my life, I have also removed what's fake. It woke me up to the state of the planet, but unexpectedly, it was also a wake up to who I had become. I want to thank you for coming along this journey and I hope you've had your own wake-up call or two. Newton's Third Law of Motion states that 'for every action there is an equal and opposite reaction'. This means every one of your actions will have a reaction that positively impacts the planet.

I want you to find your own 'Goldilocks' zone for living a zero waste life, one that balances your needs with that of the planet's. Remember that your individual actions matter and that their ripple effect is far more expansive than you could ever anticipate. Individually we are small, yet our collective power is big. Congratulations on changing your habits and for striving towards a zero waste life!

My journey started with a focus on *me,* and now I can see the changes that need to be made can only done by *we.* Zero waste living relies on the collective power of *we.* We can take control of plastic pollution. We can make a difference in the fight against climate change. We must be caretakers of the only planet we call home. We are all in this together.

# REFERENCES

Please go to WWW.ANITAVANDYKE.COM for the latest references

## CLIMATE CHANGE
*Before the Flood* – documentary (2016)
davidsuzuki.org
climaterealityproject.org

## FOOD WASTE
ozharvest.org
abc.net.au/news/2013-10-08/food-waste-value-australia/4993930

## FASHION
fashionrevolution.org
*The True Cost* – documentary (2015)
Capsule Wardrobe
Project 333

## MEDITATION
Calm app
Headspace app

## MINIMALISM
*The Minimalists* – documentary (2015)

## PLASTIC POLLUTION
plasticpollutioncoalition.org
take3.org

Anita Vandyke is a qualified rocket scientist (graduated with a Bachelor of Engineering – Aeronautical Space) and runs a successful Instagram account about zero waste living. She was born in Guangzhou, China, raised in Australia and currently splits her time between studying medicine in Sydney, and living with her husband in San Francisco. She regularly blogs about her passions for zero waste switches, minimalism, travel and all things green living.

# ACKNOWLEDGEMENTS

This book is for my followers, without whom it would not have been possible. The community built around my Instagram account (@rocket_science) and website (www.anitavandyke.com) has inspired and motivated me to keep fighting the good fight. Thank you always.

Thank you to the wonderful team at Penguin Random House Australia who helped me hone my voice and create this book. Lex Hirst, your contagious enthusiasm and talent with words should earn you a pay rise! Thank you for the vision you had of this book and most of all, thank you for believing in me. Thank you to Louisa Maggio for your design talents, and to Cristina Briones for polishing my words. Thank you to Melissa Stefanovski for your beautiful illustrations.

Thank you to my husband James, who is the inspiration for everything I do. He makes me want to be a better person and work harder for the future of our planet.

Of course, thank you to my Mum (Shirley) and dad (Henry) who taught me not to waste anything in my life. You are my teachers. Thank you to my brother, Alex, for keeping it real.

Thank you to my extended family, especially my in-laws, Yasmin and Kim, who have always been my biggest cheerleaders. Your endless support inspires me to always do better.

Finally, thank you to my friends. You know who you are. You have been through the tears, the laughs, the highs and the lows. They say you can't choose your family, but you can choose your friends – how lucky am I to have been chosen by you.